Priest dressed
as Anubis

Canopic jars

Body dried
in salt

Mummification was carried out in
special tents on the Nile's east bank.

ADVENTURES IN THE REAL WORLD

The story of MUMMIES

Penny Clarke

Sandy Creek
NEW YORK

An Imprint of Sterling Publishing
387 Park Avenue South
New York, NY 10016

Series creator: David Salariya
Author: Penny Clarke
Editor: Tanya Kant
Illustrations: David Antram, Mark Bergin, Ray Burrows, Chris Etheridge, Nick Hewetson, John James, Gordon Munro, Mark Peppé, Lee Peters, Carolyn Scrace, Lyn Stone and Gerald Wood
Consultant: Jacqueline Morley

ISBN 978-1-4351-5032-4 (HB)

Manufactured in Heshan, Guangdong Province, China
Lot #:
2 4 6 8 10 9 7 5 3 1
06/13

CONTENTS

ETERNAL LIFE?

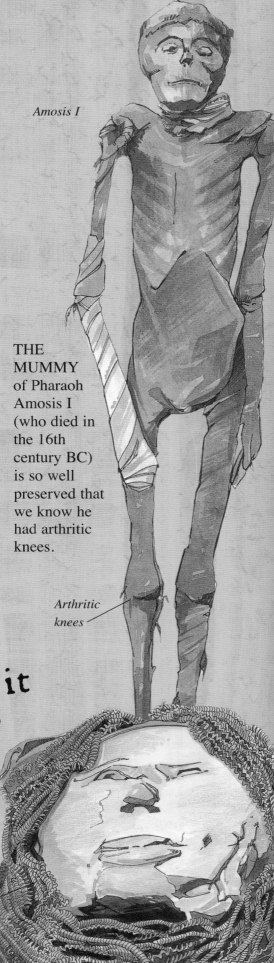

Amosis I

Name tag
identifying a
mummified
person

SAY "ANCIENT EGYPT" and
what do you think of?
Pyramids and mummies?
Pyramids were tombs for the
mummified bodies of pharaohs,
rulers of ancient Egypt. Only
pharaohs had such grand tombs, but
many people were mummified. Other civilizations built
pyramids and mummified their dead, too. But since the
Egyptian civilization lasted so long it left a lot of
pyramids and mummies for archeologists to discover.

THE
MUMMY
of Pharaoh
Amosis I
(who died in
the 16th
century BC)
is so well
preserved that
we know he
had arthritic
knees.

Lifelike?

WHY MUMMIFY (preserve)
the dead? The Egyptians
believed that people went to a
new life and that mummifying
the body would help them enjoy
it. We don't know whether the
face painted on the mummy case
flattered the person inside.

Head of
Tutankhamun

Arthritic
knees

Where did it go wrong?

THE EMBALMERS
who mummified
corpses weren't always
successful. They put so
much stuffing in Queen
Henttawy's cheeks that
her skin burst.

Queen Henttawy

4

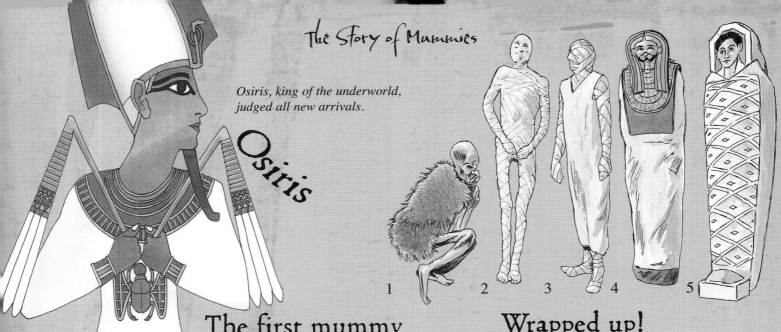

Osiris, king of the underworld, judged all new arrivals.

Osiris

1 2 3 4 5

The first mummy

THE ANCIENT EGYPTIANS believed the god **Osiris** (left) was the first mummy. Murdered by a rival, he was wrapped in bandages and became immortal. By mummifying their dead they honored them and helped them attain immortality. But the oldest known preserved Egyptian body (1) predates the Egyptians' civilization. The body was wrapped in goatskin around 3500 BC. Recorded ancient Egyptian history begins about a thousand years later.

Wrapped up!

ANCIENT EGYPT was powerful for more than two thousand years. Over time, mummies of ordinary people changed. First, bodies were just wrapped in plaster-coated linen (2). Then, in *c*.2500 BC, a linen "dress" was added (3). In the **Middle Kingdom** (c.2040–1640 BC) a painted mask covered the head and chest (4). By AD 100 Egypt was part of the Roman Empire, but mummification continued (5).

The case of the two-headed mummy?

WEALTHY PEOPLE always had more elaborate mummy cases (below) than ordinary people. But by around 300 BC displays of wealth on the coffin were more important than skillful embalming. The lady in this coffin has a lovely portrait on the outside, but there are two skulls inside (bottom)! Did the embalmers find they had a skull they couldn't identify and hide their guilty secret? Sometimes X-raying ancient artifacts provides more questions than answers!

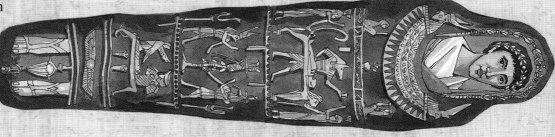

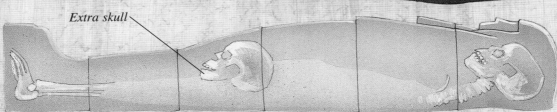

Extra skull

DEATH AND BURIAL

Body buried in a reed coffin

THE ANCIENT Egyptians believed everyone had a **ba** and a **ka**. The ba formed a person's character and the ka gave them life. When a person died, their ka did not—it remained in the body. So it was important to preserve the body as a home for the ka. Otherwise the dead person would cause bad luck for their remaining family on earth. Preserving bodies was a complicated and expensive process. The splendid mummies and lavish treasures in this book were only for the rich. Perhaps poor people, who had worked hard all their lives, were less excited about an afterlife!

AT FIRST ONLY the rich were mummified. Poor people were buried in pits in the sand (above). Egypt's climate is hot and dry, and these bodies soon dried out naturally. All that remained was a skeleton covered in tough, leathery skin —a natural mummy. Rich families might as well have saved their money, because their mummified bodies just rotted. But this changed as the art of mummification became better.

Only the rich had tombs

How much?!

GRAND TOMBS were only for the rich. Most people were buried in their village's cemetery with a few possessions to help them in their new life.

Workman crafting stone with wooden mallet

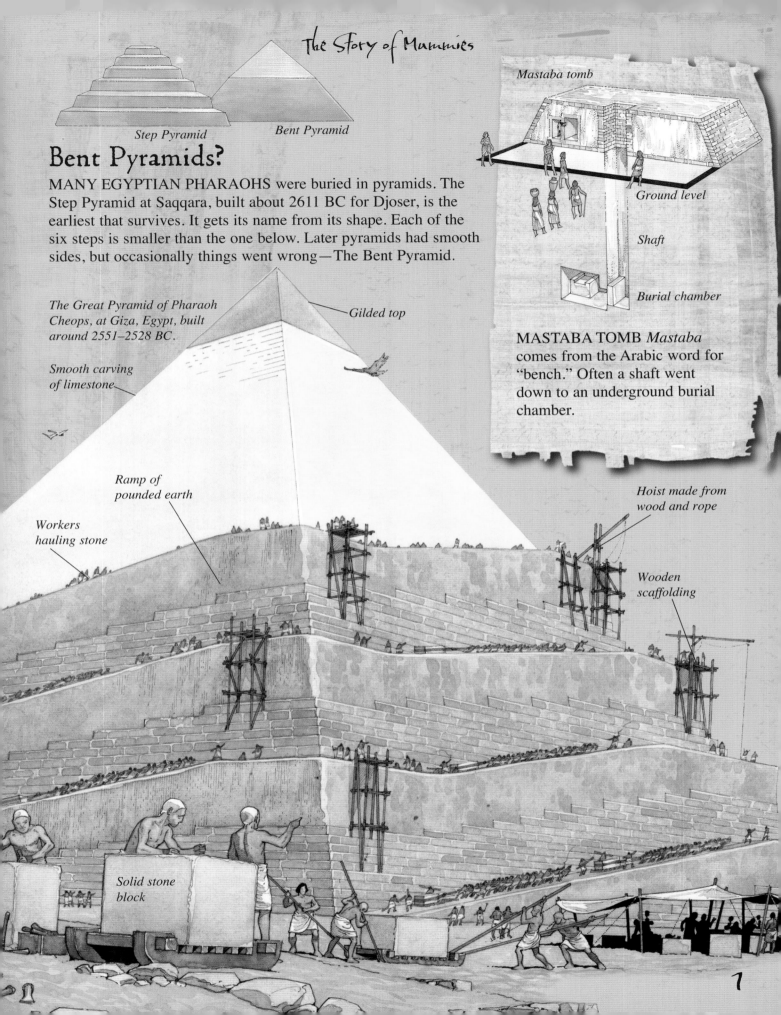

Step Pyramid

Bent Pyramid

Bent Pyramids?

MANY EGYPTIAN PHARAOHS were buried in pyramids. The Step Pyramid at Saqqara, built about 2611 BC for Djoser, is the earliest that survives. It gets its name from its shape. Each of the six steps is smaller than the one below. Later pyramids had smooth sides, but occasionally things went wrong—The Bent Pyramid.

The Great Pyramid of Pharaoh Cheops, at Giza, Egypt, built around 2551–2528 BC.

Gilded top

Smooth carving of limestone

Ramp of pounded earth

Workers hauling stone

Solid stone block

Mastaba tomb

Ground level

Shaft

Burial chamber

MASTABA TOMB *Mastaba* comes from the Arabic word for "bench." Often a shaft went down to an underground burial chamber.

Hoist made from wood and rope

Wooden scaffolding

7

A HOME FOR ETERNITY

D ETERMINED NOT TO DIE, the pharaohs ordered the building of tombs as homes for their bodies and their ka. Some pharaohs built pyramids that still survive, although their bodies and treasures were looted long ago. Archeology and modern technology have shown just how complex the pyramids' interiors were. But before entering the pyramid, priests went to a temple built against its east wall. Here they performed sacred rituals to keep the pharaoh's ka alive. This is a view of the tomb of the pharaoh Unas, who lived around 2300 BC.

Priests carried out daily ceremonies in the chapel

Statue of pharaoh

SEVERAL ENORMOUS statues, all representing the pharaoh, were placed in the mortuary temple.

Inside the tomb

A covered pathway linked the temple at the entrance of the pyramid complex to the pyramid itself.

Priests who have carried the pharaoh's coffin return to the entrance temple.

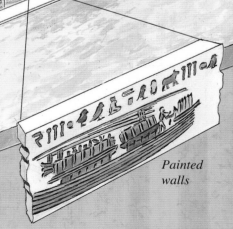

Painted walls

The River Nile

THE NILE really was Egypt's lifeblood. Its annual spring flood covered the ground with fertile **silt**, ensuring good crops and plenty of food. It was also the country's highway. So it's not surprising the pharaoh's last journey in this life was along the Nile to his tomb.

THE WALLS of the covered pathway were brightly painted. They showed sacred scenes and pictures of the pharaoh's life— especially his victories in battle.

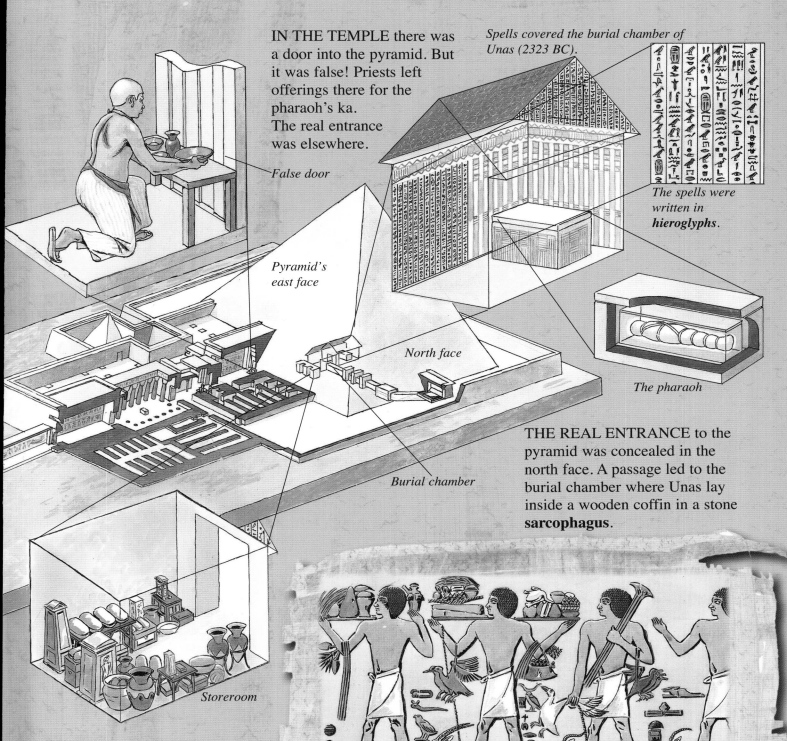

IN THE TEMPLE there was a door into the pyramid. But it was false! Priests left offerings there for the pharaoh's ka. The real entrance was elsewhere.

False door

Pyramid's east face

Spells covered the burial chamber of Unas (2323 BC).

*The spells were written in **hieroglyphs**.*

North face

The pharaoh

Burial chamber

THE REAL ENTRANCE to the pyramid was concealed in the north face. A passage led to the burial chamber where Unas lay inside a wooden coffin in a stone **sarcophagus**.

Storeroom

A Material World

CLOSE TO THE burial chamber were storerooms. These were packed with everything the pharaoh would need in his new life. And, being a ruler, he needed lots of top-quality things!

THE PHARAOH'S ka needed looking after. In this painted tomb carving a procession of servants brings offerings for the ka. After prayers and blessings, priests prepared a ritual meal from the offerings of meat, poultry, fruit, and vegetables. Then they put it in front of the pyramid's false door for the ka to enjoy.

PREPARING THE BODY

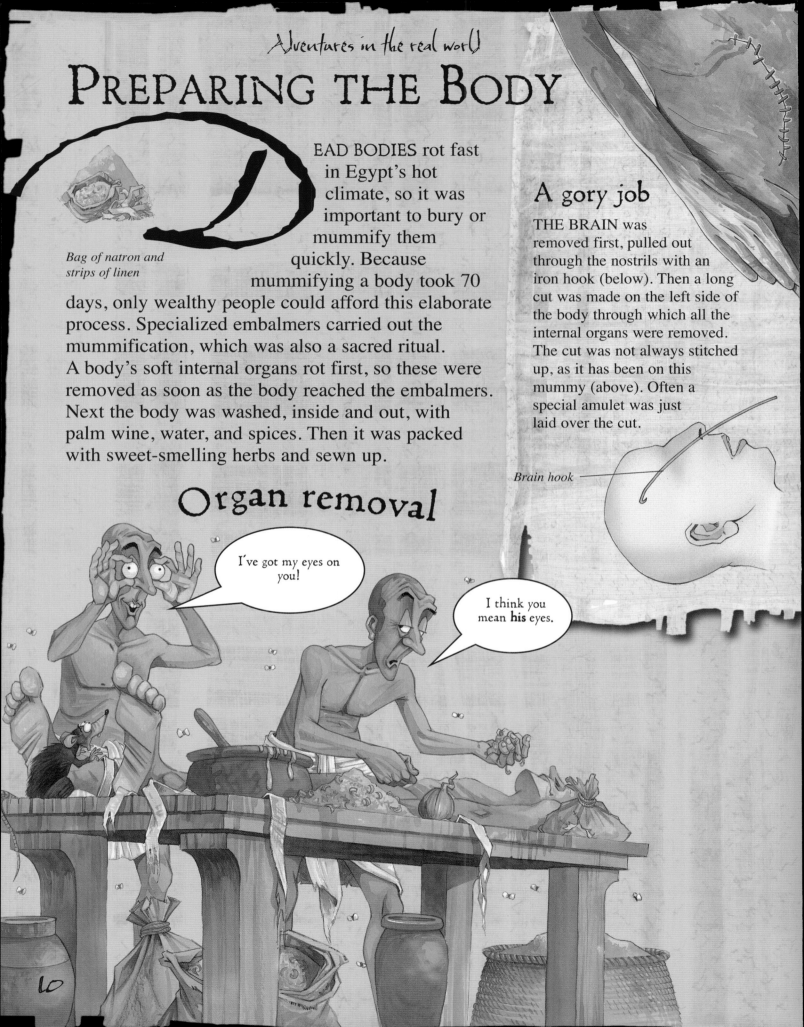

Bag of natron and strips of linen

DEAD BODIES rot fast in Egypt's hot climate, so it was important to bury or mummify them quickly. Because mummifying a body took 70 days, only wealthy people could afford this elaborate process. Specialized embalmers carried out the mummification, which was also a sacred ritual. A body's soft internal organs rot first, so these were removed as soon as the body reached the embalmers. Next the body was washed, inside and out, with palm wine, water, and spices. Then it was packed with sweet-smelling herbs and sewn up.

A gory job

THE BRAIN was removed first, pulled out through the nostrils with an iron hook (below). Then a long cut was made on the left side of the body through which all the internal organs were removed. The cut was not always stitched up, as it has been on this mummy (above). Often a special amulet was just laid over the cut.

Brain hook

Organ removal

I've got my eyes on you!

I think you mean **his** eyes.

Flint knife

All dried out

THE EMBALMERS used
flint knives (above) to cut
open the body. Once the
body was as clean as
possible it was put in a
bath and covered with
natron, a type of
natural salt (below).
Then it was left for
40 days. This dried
out the body, which
was very important
—any moisture left
in it would make
the body rot. After
40 days the skin
was like leather.

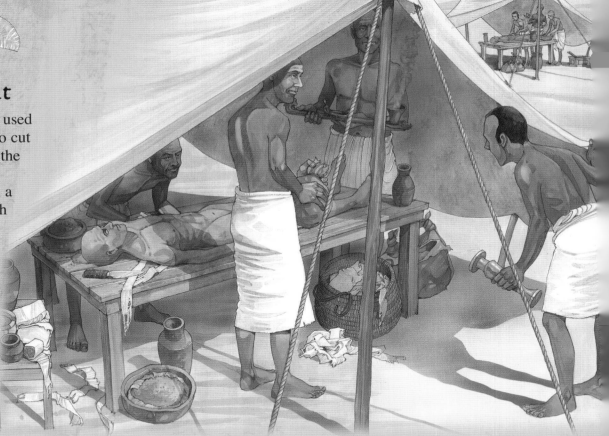

Natron bath

Salts

NEXT THE embalmers had to
make the stiff, leathery figure
look lifelike again (above). First
they rubbed it with oil to make
the skin supple. At this stage, the
body was flat and shrunken.
Packing it with sawdust and
linen pads soon made it look
more lifelike. Melted **resin** was
poured into the skull through the
nostrils, the eyelids were pulled
over the eyes and each one
covered with an **amulet**.
Now the body was ready
for wrapping.

Wall paintings

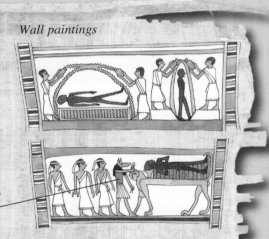

Every picture tells a (hi)story

FROM THE PAINTINGS decorating the walls of their tombs, we
have learned a great deal about the ancient Egyptians' lives and
ceremonies. In the upper picture (right) priests wash a body and pour
water over its head. Then the body is put on a couch (right, below).
A priest dressed as **Anubis**, the jackal-headed god of the underworld,
reads prayers over it.

Anubis

WELL WRAPPED UP

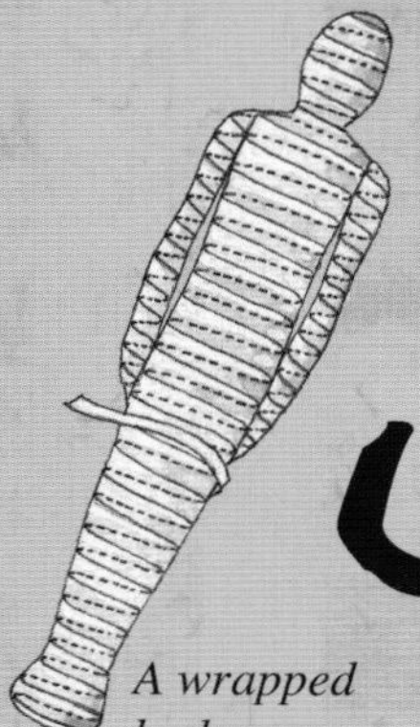

THE PRIESTS used long strips of linen cloth to wrap a body. Linen was expensive, so old cloth might be torn into strips and reused—but never for a pharaoh. Wrapping was done in a strict order; doing it any other way might bring bad luck. As they wrapped, the priests chanted prayers for the person's good health in the next world. If the arms or legs looked too thin they put padding under the strips. Everyone wanted to look their best for their next life.

A wrapped body

Gold sandal with toe thong worn by Tutankhamun

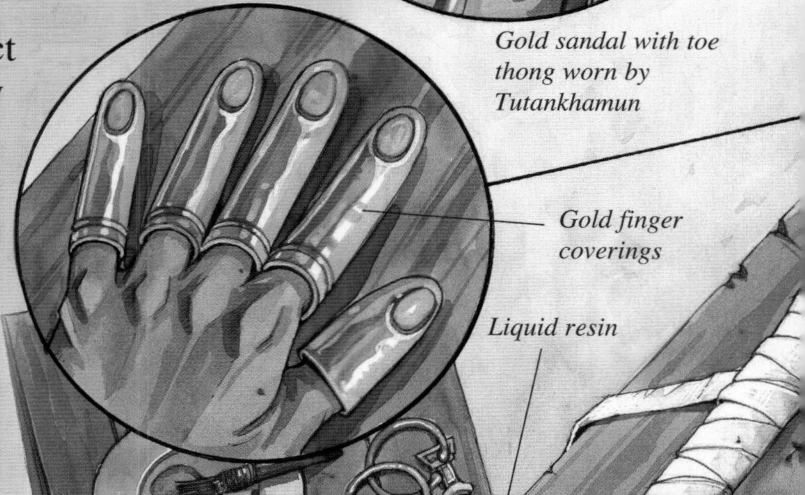

Gold finger coverings

Liquid resin

Rolls of linen

Linen to wrap the mummy

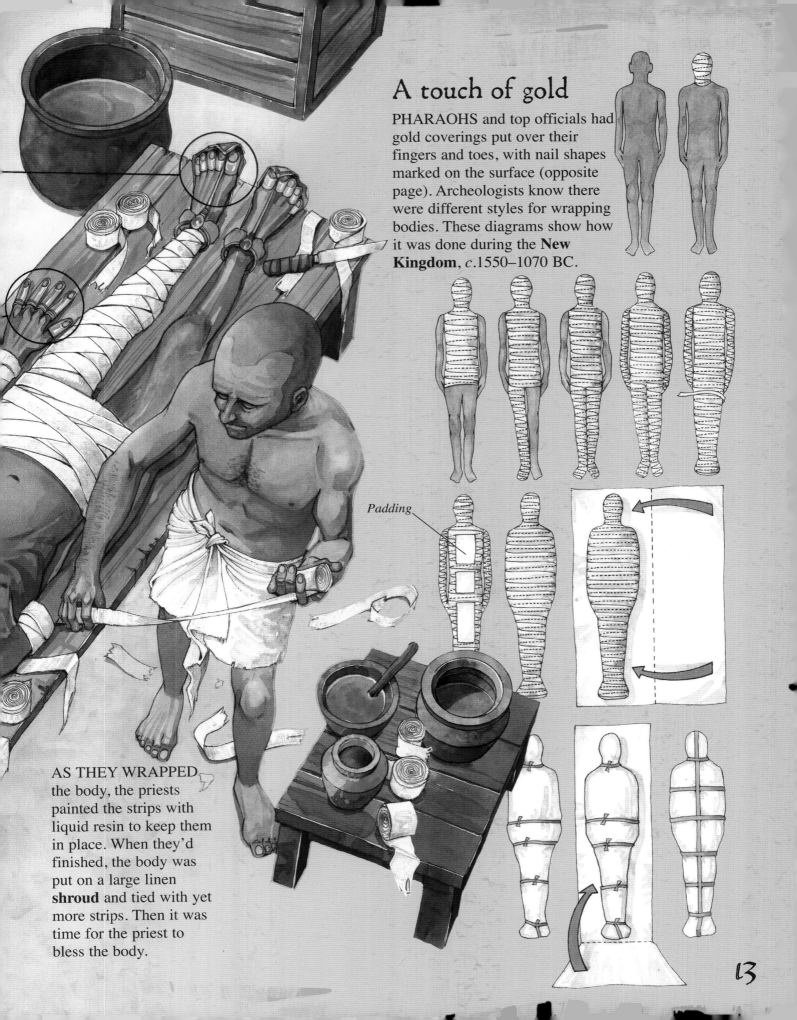

A touch of gold

PHARAOHS and top officials had gold coverings put over their fingers and toes, with nail shapes marked on the surface (opposite page). Archeologists know there were different styles for wrapping bodies. These diagrams show how it was done during the **New Kingdom**, *c*.1550–1070 BC.

Padding

AS THEY WRAPPED the body, the priests painted the strips with liquid resin to keep them in place. When they'd finished, the body was put on a large linen **shroud** and tied with yet more strips. Then it was time for the priest to bless the body.

13

A CHARMED LIFE?

Amulet of the eye of Ra, the Sun God

THE PRIESTS slipped amulets between the linen strips as they wrapped. These would help to protect the dead person in his or her new life. But the journey there was difficult. The amulets represented the Egyptian gods who would help the dead on their way and protect them from harm.

Gold-leaf tongue

Gold eye

Added extras

THE ANCIENT Egyptians believed the next life was a continuation of this one. So it was important to maintain your position in society. This meant having a mummy that showed how rich you were. You might want a tongue of gold leaf and delicate gold "eyes" to put in your eye sockets (above).

Ready for the underworld?

> BOO!

> Take that off—this isn't a costume party!

Anubis, Keeper of the Dead

A PRIEST DRESSED as the jackal-headed god Anubis supervises the wrapping of a body. Jackals are scavengers and eat dead bodies, which is important in hot climates because otherwise bodies would rot and cause disease. Jackals were common in Egypt and were associated with death, and so a jackal was worshipped as god of the underworld.

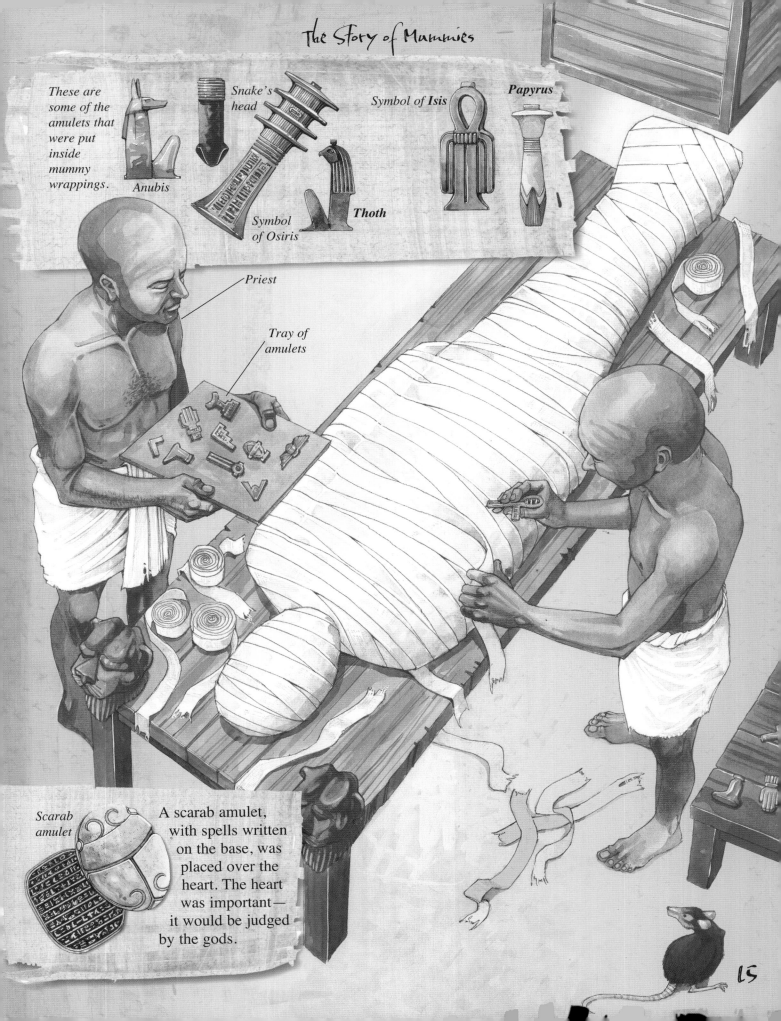

These are some of the amulets that were put inside mummy wrappings.

Anubis

Snake's head

Symbol of Osiris

Thoth

Symbol of **Isis**

Papyrus

Priest

Tray of amulets

Scarab amulet

A scarab amulet, with spells written on the base, was placed over the heart. The heart was important— it would be judged by the gods.

AMULETS FOR A PHARAOH

JUTANKHAMUN ruled Egypt from 1333 to 1323 BC. He was not an important pharaoh in the history of ancient Egypt. But for us, and our knowledge of the Egyptians, he is of enormous importance. His tomb astonished Howard Carter and his team when they discovered it in 1922. There were hidden treasures, too: 150 amulets came to light when Carter and his helpers carefully removed the pharaoh's linen wrappings.

The ankh, an ancient Egyptian symbol of life

GUIDANCE on where to place the amulets could be found in the **Book of the Dead**. This sacred text described all the rituals needed to keep the dead safe.

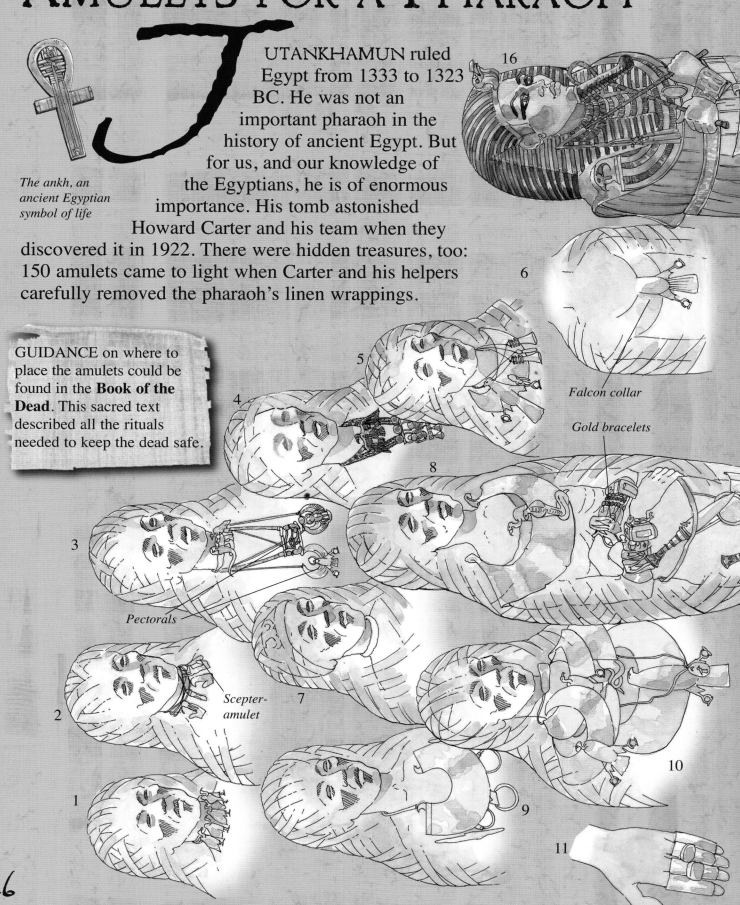

Falcon collar

Gold bracelets

Pectorals

Scepter-amulet

The pharaoh's charms

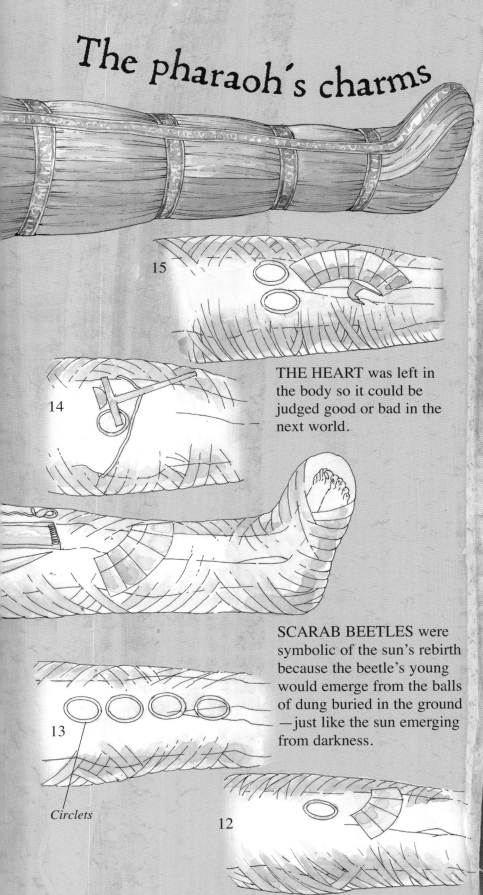

15

14

THE HEART was left in the body so it could be judged good or bad in the next world.

13

Circlets

12

SCARAB BEETLES were symbolic of the sun's rebirth because the beetle's young would emerge from the balls of dung buried in the ground —just like the sun emerging from darkness.

AMULETS MOSTLY consisted of tiny figures of the gods or symbols of them. For example, a pillar-shaped *djed* amulet represented Osiris and a knotlike amulet or *tyet* represented his wife Isis. The god **Horus** was shown by a falcon. Tutankhamun's amulets were the same as those of other Egyptians but, as a pharaoh, he had more of them and his amulets were finer than anyone else's.

1 Vultures—symbols of **Upper Egypt**
2 Thoth, serpent's head, falcon's head, Anubis, and scepter-amulet
3 At the neck: cobras, vulture; pectorals (amulets put on the chest): sacred eye, scarab, falcon
4 Scarab and vulture pectorals
5 Vulture collar, scepter, djed pillar, tyet knot
6 Falcon collar
7 Beadwork cap under linen wrappings
8 Cobra, falcon, and vulture collars, bracelets, girdle, daggers, apron
9 Collar
10 Collars, pectoral
11 Finger stalls, signet rings
12 Circlet, collar
13 Circlets
14 Girdle, circlet, T-shaped amulet
15 Circlets, collar
16 Tutankhamun's mummy with a portrait mask of the pharaoh. On his head are the vulture of Nekhbet and the cobra of Wadjit. They were the symbols of Upper and **Lower Egypt**, the two parts of his kingdom. In his hands are the royal flail and crook, and below them a golden bird represents his ba.

A GOLDEN SHRINE

Scarab amulets were placed over the heart

WHEN THE mummification process began, the pharaoh's internal organs were removed—to stop them rotting and destroying his mummy. But they weren't thrown away. They too were mummified and placed in tiny coffins called **Canopic jars**. All mummies had their organs removed and put in Canopic jars, but only a pharaoh's Canopic jars were put in a golden shrine (right). At the top of the shrine sun disks rest on the heads of rearing cobras, the symbols of the pharaoh's royal power. On each side, the four guardian goddesses of Egypt stretch out their arms to protect the shrine.

Not for the faint-hearted!

Shrine on its sledge

Where shall I put all of this?

In the jar with the hawk head.

What a job!

EMBALMING AND preparing a body for mummification was a really unpleasant, smelly task. Only specially trained priests were allowed to carry out this work because it had to be done carefully and without damaging the body or its organs. The ancient Egyptians believed that the dead person would need his or her body and its "contents" again in the afterlife.

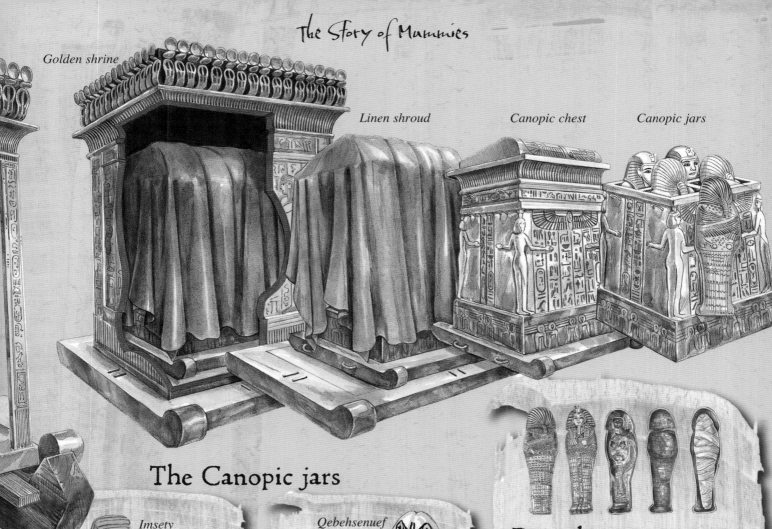

Golden shrine

Linen shroud

Canopic chest

Canopic jars

The Canopic jars

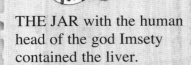

Imsety

THE JAR with the human head of the god Imsety contained the liver.

Qebehsenuef

INTESTINES were put in the jar with the hawk head of the god Qebehsenuef.

Duamutef

THE JAR for the stomach was topped with the jackal head of Duamutef.

Hapy

THE JAR for the lungs had a top like an ape, representing the god Hapy.

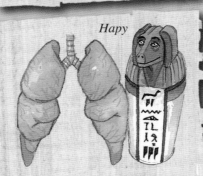

Prized possessions

THE TOPS of the Canopic jars represented the four sons of the god Horus. But pharaohs were special—as Howard Carter found in 1922, when he discovered the tomb of Pharaoh Tutankhamun. His organs had been wrapped in linen strips, just like the body, and put in jars shaped like tiny golden coffins— miniature versions of his own. These jars were put in a chest carved from semiprecious **quartzite**. A linen cloth was placed over this chest and it was put in the golden shrine (above). A statue of Anubis was left to guard the shrine. And that is where Carter found it more than 3,000 years later.

MAKING THE COFFIN

The sacred falcon, from the Book of the Dead.

WHILE A BODY was being mummified, carpenters would make its coffin. Over the centuries, the ancient Egyptians' burial customs changed and developed. But one thing remained constant: the richer you were, the finer your coffin.

Coffin craft

AFTER THE COFFIN had been carved it was painted with gesso, a mixture of chalk and glue. Then the craftsman pressed on thin sheets of gold (left).

COLORED GLASS was used for details such as eyes. On the best coffins the body was covered in a thick layer of gesso in which fine details were carved.

The pharaoh's dead cat owns more gold than I do!

THROUGHOUT ANCIENT EGYPT the workshops of embalmers and coffin makers were busy places. As well as human bodies, they mummified the bodies of animals, such as cats and baboons, which were sacred to the Egyptians.

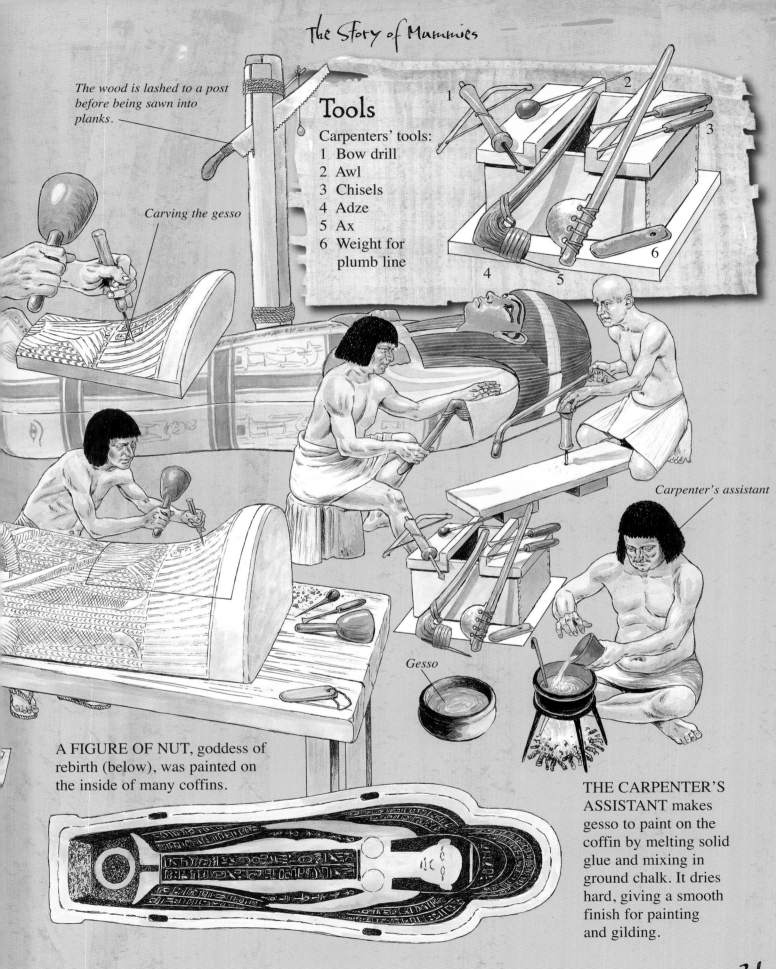

The wood is lashed to a post before being sawn into planks.

Carving the gesso

Tools

Carpenters' tools:
1. Bow drill
2. Awl
3. Chisels
4. Adze
5. Ax
6. Weight for plumb line

Carpenter's assistant

Gesso

A FIGURE OF NUT, goddess of rebirth (below), was painted on the inside of many coffins.

THE CARPENTER'S ASSISTANT makes gesso to paint on the coffin by melting solid glue and mixing in ground chalk. It dries hard, giving a smooth finish for painting and gilding.

INTO THE COFFIN

WHEN THE MUMMY was ready and the coffins finished, it was time for the next stage of the journey to the afterlife. Early Egyptian coffins were simple rectangular wooden boxes, with a few prayers painted on them. But by the Middle Kingdom, as these pictures show, coffins had become very elaborate. Each one was shaped like a mummified human body. Pharaohs and other important officials had up to three mummy-shaped coffins, each one fitting snugly inside the previous one.

Anubis, the jackal-headed god of the underworld

The face of Death?

THE FACES on coffin lids show an idealized human waiting for their new life. They are not portraits of the person inside.

One body, three coffins

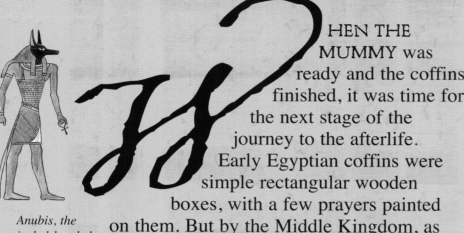

These three coffins are the finest in Egypt.

Let's hope the gods think so.

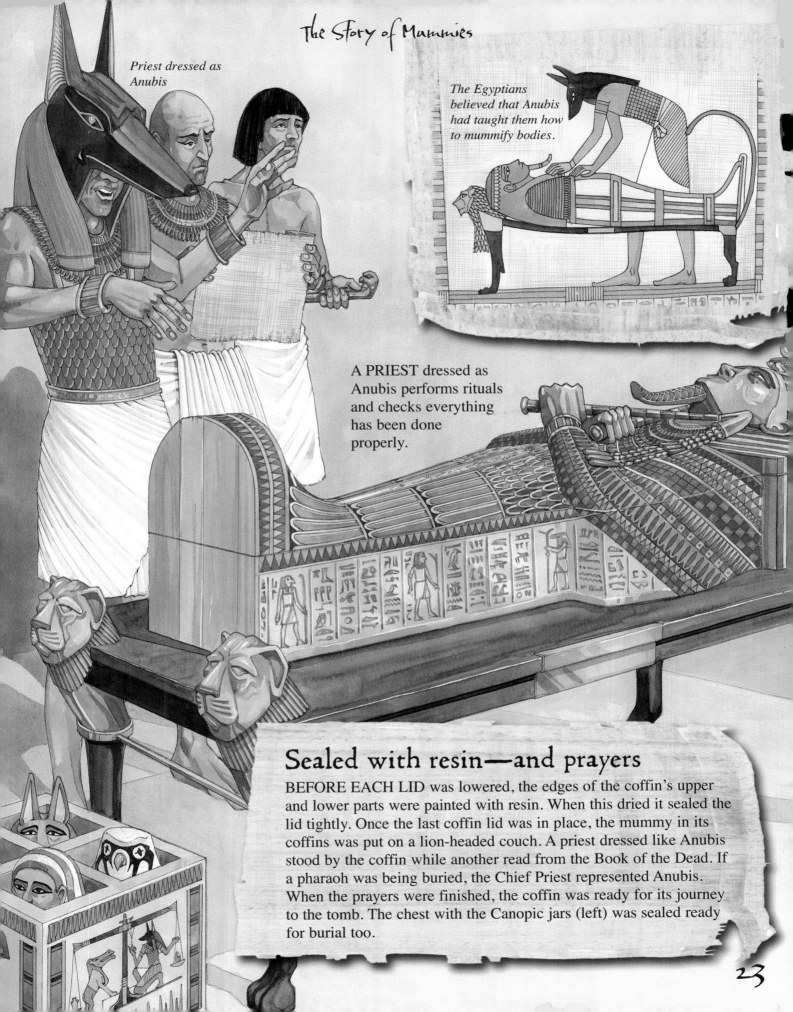

Priest dressed as Anubis

The Egyptians believed that Anubis had taught them how to mummify bodies.

A PRIEST dressed as Anubis performs rituals and checks everything has been done properly.

Sealed with resin—and prayers

BEFORE EACH LID was lowered, the edges of the coffin's upper and lower parts were painted with resin. When this dried it sealed the lid tightly. Once the last coffin lid was in place, the mummy in its coffins was put on a lion-headed couch. A priest dressed like Anubis stood by the coffin while another read from the Book of the Dead. If a pharaoh was being buried, the Chief Priest represented Anubis. When the prayers were finished, the coffin was ready for its journey to the tomb. The chest with the Canopic jars (left) was sealed ready for burial too.

23

COFFINS AND SHRINES

*U*NLIKE MOST OTHER pharaohs' burial chambers, Tutankhamun's still contained all its treasures when it was discovered in 1922. This is why we know so much about his burial. Tutankhamun was not a very powerful pharaoh, so archeologists assume that all pharaohs must have had magnificent tombs. Tutankhamun's mummy was put into several coffins and the sarcophagus was placed inside several shrines. The shrines were as magnificent as the coffins. They were made of gilded wood and decorated with many prayers.

Thoth, the ibis-headed god

Detailed designs

THE CASE OF THE FIRST (outer) coffin was made of wood covered in gesso. The decorations carved in this layer showed through the gold covering it.

Second coffin

Third coffin

Tutankhamun's mummy

Layers of coffins

Each coffin revealed another even more magnificent one. The first gold-covered coffin had been marked with a pattern of feathers. The second one was decorated with gold, colored glass, **faience**, and semiprecious stones. But the third coffin was the most spectacular—it was made of solid gold.

The lower parts of the three coffins

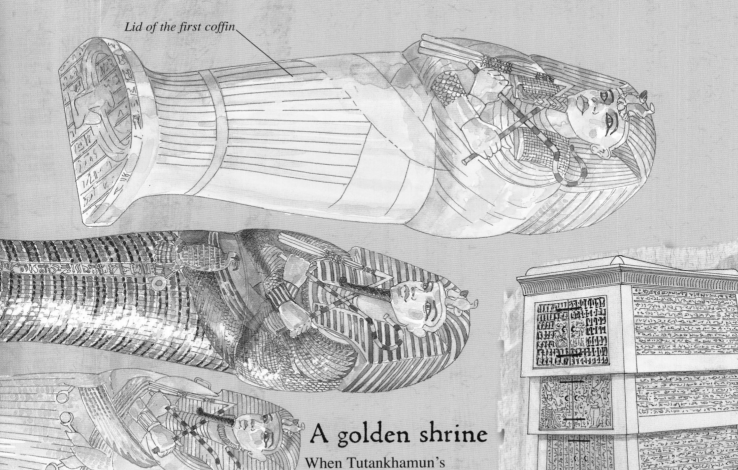

Lid of the first coffin

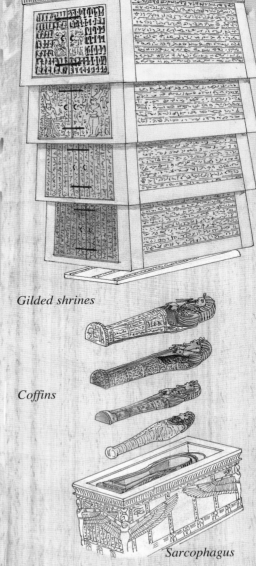

Gilded shrines

Coffins

Sarcophagus

A golden shrine

When Tutankhamun's tomb was discovered there seemed to be one magnificent golden shrine. This was amazing enough, but inside were three others (right). All were made of wood covered in gold and richly decorated. Under the fourth and final shrine lay the stone sarcophagus.

Tutankhamun revealed

HOWARD CARTER, who had worked in Egypt as an archeologist for many years, had an idea of what was inside the stone sarcophagus. On February 12, 1924 the lid was lifted. The linen shroud was removed and there lay the first coffin in all its golden magnificence: covered in a pattern of feathers, the hands holding the royal crook and flail.

TO THE TOMB

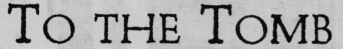

Instruments for the Opening of the Mouth ceremony

WHEN THE LAST coffin was sealed, it was time for the journey to the tomb. A canopy stood ready on a boat-shaped sledge. Once the coffin had been placed under the canopy, the sledge was dragged to the dead person's home. There the family joined the funeral procession as it headed for the banks of the Nile. The coffin was transferred to a boat and launched on the river. The west, where the sun set, was sacred to the Egyptians, so all burials were on the Nile's west bank.

Supplies for the afterlife

IN THE TOMB on the west bank the stone sarcophagus awaited the coffin. Also there were supplies for the dead person: clothes, furniture, food, drink, jewelry, chariots, and servants. Fortunately for the deceased's real servants, those in the tomb were little pottery models called *shabti*. The richer the dead person, the more possessions and shabti were put in the tomb. Ordinary people were also buried with possessions, but theirs were far fewer and simpler.

A CROWD of people brought gifts and goods to put in the tomb. **Professional mourners**, *paid to grieve for the dead, wailed their mourning* **dirges**.

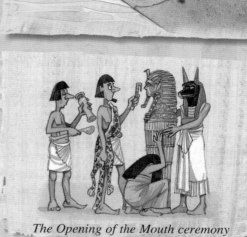

The Opening of the Mouth ceremony

> Who are we wailing for again?

Procession across the river Nile

ONCE ACROSS THE NILE, the coffin in its shrine was put on another sledge and dragged to the tomb (below). There, in front of a priest dressed as Anubis, the dead person's ears, eyes, nose, and mouth were "opened" to reawaken the mummy's senses (opposite page). If this was not done, he or she could not "live" in the next world.

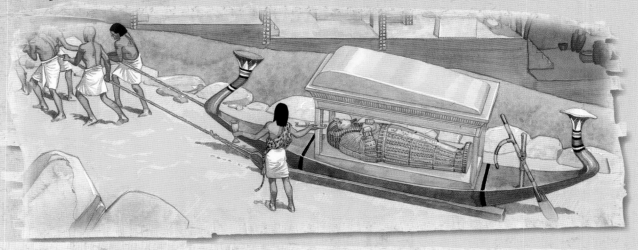

Thoth

Ma'at

Anubis

Ammut

Judgment day

BEFORE A MUMMY could enter the underworld, its heart was weighed against the feather of Ma'at, the goddess of truth (left). Then the dead person had to swear before 42 judges, including the gods, that they had led a good life. If they passed the test, they entered the underworld.

27

A TOMB FOR A GOD

JO THEIR PEOPLE, the pharaohs were gods. During their lives pharaohs protected Egypt from its enemies, and they would continue to do so after they died, but from the next world. It was therefore right that pharaohs had the best of everything in their tombs. In 1922 Howard Carter had the first glimpse inside Tutankhamun's tomb since it was sealed in 1323 BC. Asked what he could see, he replied: "Wonderful things." That must be one of the biggest understatements ever!

Food found in Tutankhamun's tomb

Buried Ship

BOATS PLAYED such an important part in the lives of the Egyptians that they were sometimes put in tombs. Most tomb chambers were too small for a finished boat, so a partly built boat was put in, together with everything needed to finish it.

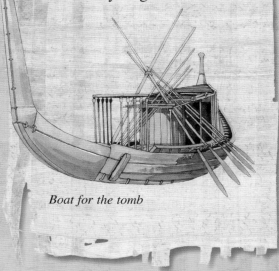

Boat for the tomb

Gifts for a God

WE KNOW FROM photographs that everything shown here was in Tutankhamun's tomb when Carter found it. What we don't know is what procedures took place as the tomb was set up.

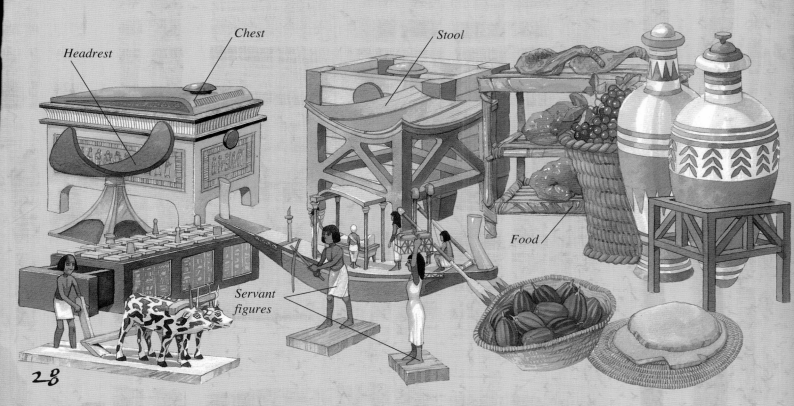

Headrest

Chest

Stool

Food

Servant figures

28

THERE MUST have been an important official in charge of filling the tomb, a **scribe** with a list of all the objects, and sweating servants to carry them in. Was the atmosphere tense? After all, this was important work and the gods were bound to be watching.

GRAND DESIGNS

The coffins were placed in the sarcophagus, with a linen cloth drawn over them

THE TOMBS of pharaohs were so big and complicated that work began long before a pharaoh died. Most pharaohs took part in planning their own tomb, to be sure it was big and grand enough. Once all the main chambers had been excavated, a huge block of stone for the pharaoh's sarcophagus was taken down into the burial chamber. This was a difficult task, and probably caused many accidents. Once it was in place, the stonemasons and sculptors started work. All surfaces of the sarcophagus were decorated with sacred texts and images of the gods. These would help the pharaoh on his journey in the afterlife, where he would be a god himself.

Meeting a deadline?

THE WALLS OF THE TOMB were as decorative as the sides of the sarcophagus. But this was not just interior decoration—it was to ensure the pharaoh had a safe journey into the afterlife. The men working on the tomb had a difficult task: the tomb must be ready when the pharaoh died, but when would that be? He might be in good health, but then have a hunting accident or die of a sudden illness. Life was short in ancient Egypt; few people reached 40— and pharaohs were no exception.

Egyptian artists' tools

Tuthmosis III

THE SARCOPHAGUS of Tuthmosis III (c.1425 BC) was carved out of yellow quartzite, painted red. As the sculptors chiseled out the sacred texts, the yellow quartzite was revealed through the red paint. Then black and white highlights were added.

Entrance

INSIDE THE TOMB, reaching the burial chamber was difficult. Steps, stairs, and twisting passages were designed to keep the pharaoh safe from tomb robbers.

Burial chamber

Storeroom

Walls decorated with protective spells

33

DISCOVERING WONDERS

URING THE PERIOD that archeologists call the "New Kingdom," the pharaohs were buried in the Valley of the Kings. Around 1085 BC, Egypt's power and wealth began to decline. The country was attacked by enemies that it was too weak to defeat. The Valley of the Kings was abandoned. Slowly the pharaohs' burial ground, hidden under deep sand and fallen rock, was forgotten.

THANKS TO technology developed long after Carter examined Tutankhamun's mummy in 1925, we now know that the pharaoh was around 17 when he died c.1323 BC.

CARTER AND HIS team worked for ten years in the tomb. Everything was recorded and photographed before it went to Cairo Museum.

Scientists examining a mummy

Bead and flower collar worn by Tutankhamun's mummy

THE VALLEY of the Kings was rediscovered by Howard Carter, working for the wealthy Englishman Lord Carnarvon.

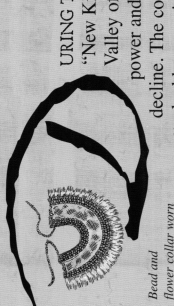
Howard Carter

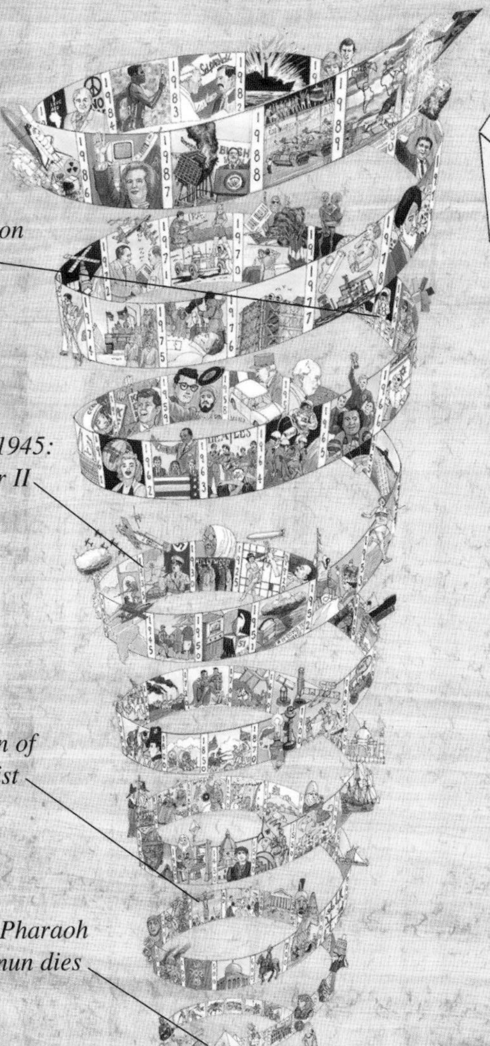

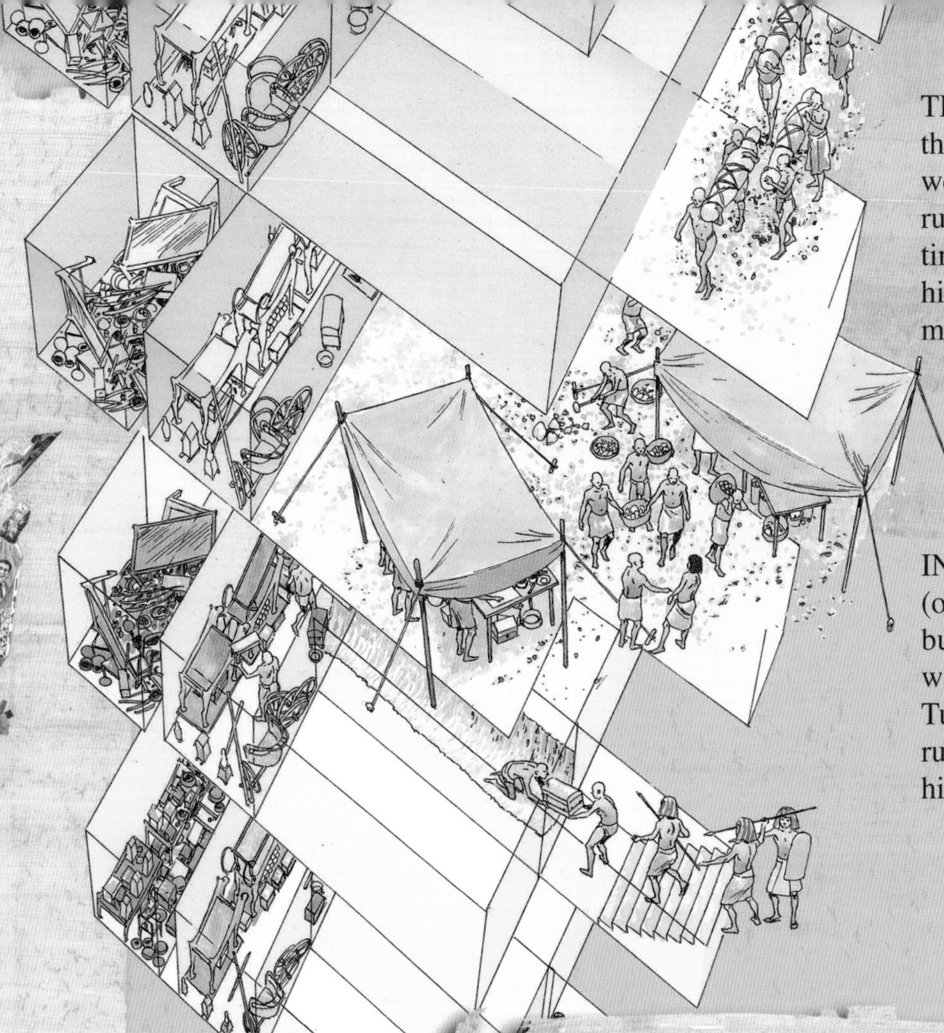

THE ENTRANCE to the tomb had been well disguised by rubble in ancient times. By 1922 it was hidden further by more rocks and sand.

IN 1151 BC Ramses (or Ramesses) V was buried. His tomb was so close to Tutankhamun's that rubble from it helped hide the earlier tomb.

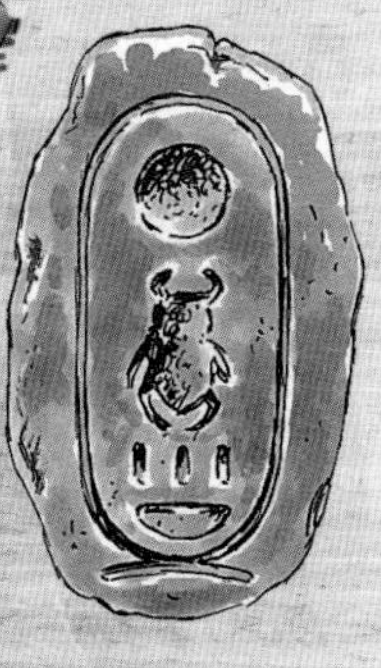

Left to rest?

WHEN THE ceremonies were over, priests closed the tomb's door, sealing it with Tutankhamun's seal (left) so he could rest undisturbed. But did he?

CARTER'S ONLY clue to the whereabouts of the tomb was a cup with Tutankhamun's name on it, found nearby a few years earlier.

Timeline of discoveries

The time spiral below shows just how long ago Tutankhamun lived. The discovery of his tomb 3,000 years later has made the long-dead young pharaoh more famous than he ever was in his lifetime.

AD 1969:
First man on
the moon

AD 1939–1945:
World War II

AD 30:
Crucifixion of
Jesus Christ

1323 BC: Pharaoh
Tutankhamun dies

TOMB ROBBERY!

Hieroglyph of an Egyptian punishment— being impaled on a stake

EVERY EGYPTIAN pharaoh and his officials feared that the treasures in the tomb would be targeted by robbers. And they were right: few tombs escaped this unwanted attention. As soon as he saw the entrance door of Tutankhamun's tomb, Carter knew that it, too, had been broken into. In fact robbers had broken in twice, the first time only a few years after he was buried. They had broken the seal on the outer shrine and taken most of the movable treasures from the other chambers. But nothing was missing from the burial chamber— perhaps they were disturbed before they could get in.

Hidden treasures

EVERYONE who planned a grand tomb full of gold and other treasures did their best to protect it from robbers, but they rarely succeeded. Even though robbing a tomb was a crime punished by a terrible death, the lure of all that treasure was just too great. What did the robbers do with their booty? We don't know, but they probably hid the evidence by melting down the gold and selling it on to make more treasures—and perhaps they would be robbed too!

Breaking and entering

Go for the glass and linen—it's more valuable than gold!

Let's take everything to be on the safe side.

Put off by punishments?

HOW MANY tomb robbers were caught?
Not many, judging
by the number of
robbed tombs!

Thieves under arrest

35

NONHUMAN MUMMIES

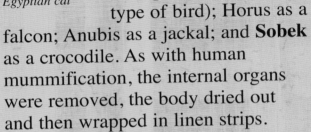

Mummy of an ancient Egyptian cat

THE EGYPTIANS didn't only mummify humans. Archeologists have discovered mummies of animals and birds. Indeed, there seem to have been whole cemeteries for animals. Why did the Egyptians do this? Perhaps because many of their gods were represented as birds and animals: for example, Thoth as an ibis (a type of bird); Horus as a falcon; Anubis as a jackal; and **Sobek** as a crocodile. As with human mummification, the internal organs were removed, the body dried out and then wrapped in linen strips.

Why animals?

THE MUMMIES of cats and crocodiles are particularly common. Did ordinary people have them in their homes, hoping these sacred creatures would look after them? Or were they bought as mummy substitutes by people too poor to have their own bodies mummified?

Is it buy one, get one free?

I should've bought a snake!

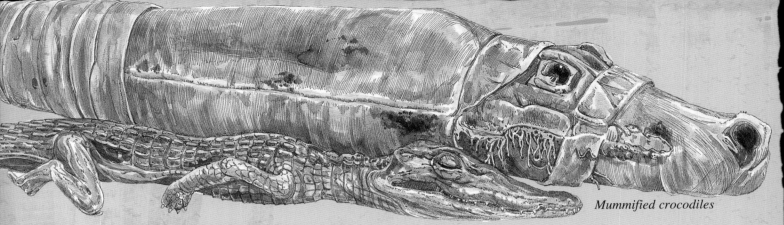
Mummified crocodiles

Crocodiles, gods of the Nile

THOUSANDS OF MUMMIFIED crocodiles (above), both wrapped and unwrapped, have been discovered. It's not surprising that a crocodile symbolized Sobek, the Egyptians' god of water, because crocodiles were very common in the Nile. And it was the river's annual flood which made the land of Egypt so rich and fertile.

Pet mummies!

MUCH-LOVED PETS were also mummified and sometimes even put in a sarcophagus. This limestone sarcophagus belonged to a prince's favorite cat. Pets belonging to ordinary people would have had wooden sarcophagi.

A royal cat's sarcophagus

Mummified baboon

Sacred creatures

BABOONS WERE very common animals and, like the ibis, were sacred to the god Thoth. The Canopic jar that held the lungs of a mummified body always had a top shaped like a baboon's head. And there are many records of baboons being kept as pets.

Ibis

Bull

Cat

A MUMMIFIED BULL from the **Old Kingdom** (*c*.2575–2134 BC) and the mummy of an ibis (above). The style of bandaging of the mummified cat (right) shows that it died about 50 BC.

THE VALLEY OF THE KINGS

HE EGYPTIAN PYRAMIDS, built mostly in the Old Kingdom, were pharaohs' tombs. They were tempting targets for robbers. Later pharaohs were buried in the less accessible Valley of the Kings. But that still didn't stop the robbers. To prevent the pharaohs from being disturbed, priests moved their mummies and buried them in secret tombs where they were not discovered until the 19th century. Their treasures remained in the original tombs and were looted thousands of years ago. Ordinary people were buried with few treasures, but robbers usually got them too.

The Valley of the Kings, burial place of the pharaohs from c.1500 BC

What's his name?

INTEREST IN ANCIENT EGYPT grew in northern Europe throughout the 19th century. Sadly, many mummies were destroyed in ignorance, being unwrapped for "entertainment."

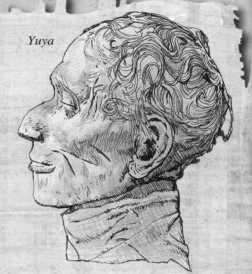

Yuya

Not a pharaoh?

YOU COULD be buried in the Valley of the Kings even if you weren't a pharaoh, but you had to be a very important person. As the parents of Queen Tiye (mother of Akhenaten, pharaoh of Egypt 1353–1336 BC), Yuya (above) and his wife Thuya were important. Their mummies are well preserved and they give a good idea of their appearance in life.

38

Queen Nodjmet's over-padded cheeks

SOMETIMES EMBALMERS tried too hard to make mummies look their best. Priests in the 10th century BC stuffed too much padding into Queen Nodjmet's cheeks—she looks very odd.

Queen Tiye

THE BEST MUMMIES give a good idea of what the living person looked like. Archeologists believe the elderly woman (above) is Queen Tiye, mother of Akhenaten. Seti I (right) passed on his military skill to his son, Ramses II.

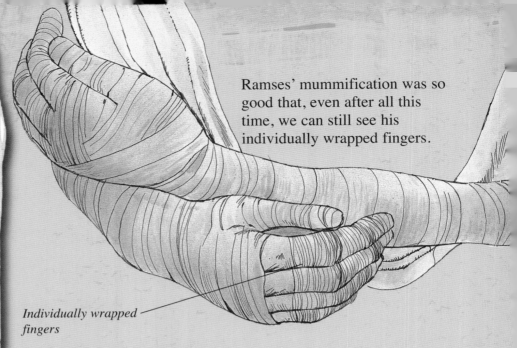

Ramses' mummification was so good that, even after all this time, we can still see his individually wrapped fingers.

Individually wrapped fingers

Perfect preservation

RAMSES (OR RAMESSES) II, WHO DIED around 1225 BC, was one of Egypt's greatest pharaohs. Originally buried in the Valley of the Kings, his mummy was later removed and hidden for safety, and so it survived. Ramses was a very popular pharaoh; he lived to be almost 90 and had many, many children.

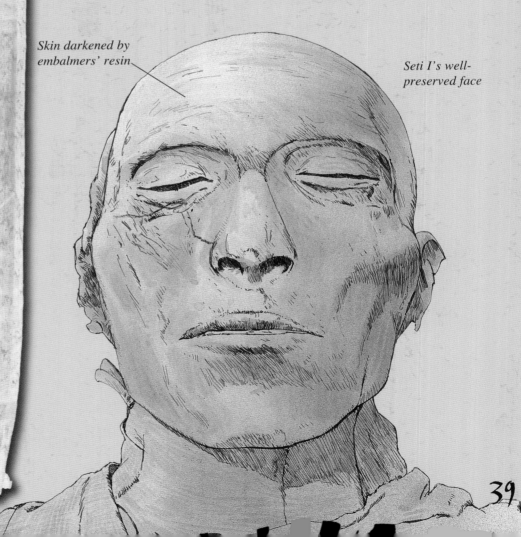

Skin darkened by embalmers' resin

Seti I's well-preserved face

THE MUMMIES' SECRETS

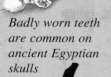

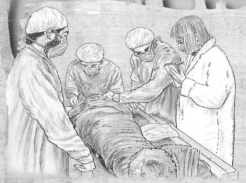

Badly worn teeth are common on ancient Egyptian skulls

TODAY'S ARCHEOLOGISTS have many technological tools to help them study ancient objects—including mummies. Most of these technologies were developed for other purposes, but archeologists quickly spotted their usefulness. The first, the discovery of X-rays in 1895, enabled archeologists to study the inside of a mummy without damaging it. Radio-carbon dating, CAT-scans (cross-sectional X-rays), and DNA testing have been added to the tool kit. Now we know family relationships, what people died of, and the illnesses they suffered.

Mummy surgery?

THE BEST WAY to find out as much as possible about a mummy is to dissect it (above). Because this destroys the mummy, it is only done on those that are already badly decayed or damaged.

Family resemblance

Seti I

Ramses II

Merenpath

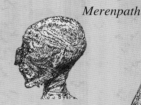

EARLY ARCHEOLOGISTS COULD only work out family relationships from distinctive features, which was rather unreliable. Now science, rather than the shape of their noses, shows (above, left to right) that Seti I was the father of Ramses II and Merenpath was Seti's grandson.

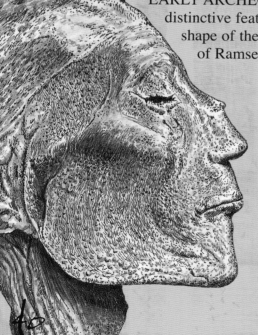

Egyptian illnesses

THE SCARS ON RAMSES V's face (left) are the result of smallpox. Polio may have caused Pharaoh Siptah's badly deformed left foot (right).

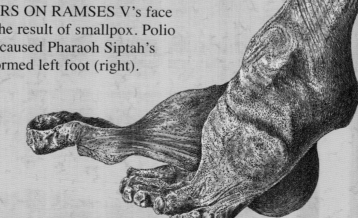

X-ray machine

CAT scanner

A grisly death

WAS SEQENENRE TAO (above) killed in battle? Certainly his mummy shows signs of a horrible death, hacked with axes and clubs. **Forensic** study shows he had been lucky to survive an earlier head wound, although it may have partially paralyzed him.

CAT SCANNERS were developed in the 1960s. These machines show a cross-section view of a mummy's contents using X-rays. Ultrasound is another method used to study mummies. Based on sound or other vibrations, it is mostly used to examine pregnant women.

Shaved head

Missing nose from bomb damage caused in 1941.

SCIENCE SHOWS the priest Natsef-Amun (right) died in his forties, that he was quite tall, and had dental problems. But there's still an unsolved mystery: why is his tongue sticking out? Two theories: he may have been bitten by an insect and his tongue swelled, or perhaps he was strangled.

Shaved chin

THIS EGYPTIAN teenager's reconstructed face looks a little odd, but it's based on fact. Manchester University's archeologists who did the work found she'd had a bone defect and may have had difficulty breathing. That's why her mouth is slightly open.

Mummy's wrappings

IS THERE A CURSE?

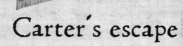

A mosquito: the true cause of the mummy's curse?

*H*OWARD CARTER'S work in Egypt was paid for by Lord Carnarvon, a wealthy English aristocrat. Carnarvon suffered from poor health and his doctors advised him to spend his winters somewhere warmer than Britain. This was what doctors usually told their rich patients to do in the early 20th century. Most of them wintered in the south of France, but Carnarvon needed somewhere warmer. He was also fascinated by archeology, and Egypt had both warmth and ancient remains.

Carter's escape

IF ANYONE was to die from a mummy's curse, it should have been Howard Carter. He broke the seals that had protected Tutankhamun for so long, and he opened the pharaoh's innermost shrine. But instead of being cursed he lived for another 17 years, and spent 10 of them working on the tomb!

Dare you open the tomb?

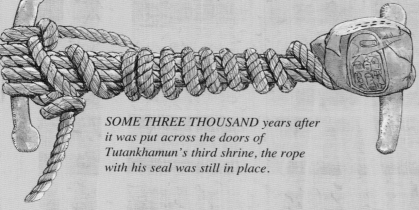

SOME THREE THOUSAND years after it was put across the doors of Tutankhamun's third shrine, the rope with his seal was still in place.

Curse or coincidence?

SOON AFTER Tutankhamun's tomb was opened, a mosquito bit Lord Carnarvon. This led to blood poisoning and then pneumonia. A healthy person would probably have survived, but Carnarvon, already in poor health, died. His death was almost as big a sensation as the tomb's discovery. Had the mummy cursed him?

I should have brought some repellent...

The Story of Mummies

Mummy medicines

A TRADE IN GOODS stolen from tombs grew up between Egypt and Europe, and these goods included mummies. No one then realized their significance, and many mummies were ground up by phony doctors for "medicines." Nobody knows what happened to their patients, but the curse doesn't seem to have affected these quack doctors.

IF THERE REALLY was a curse on anyone disturbing these tombs, surely the ancient Egyptians themselves would have feared it? But all the tomb robberies show that they didn't.

FROM THE LATE 17th century an increasing number of European tourists visited Egypt. Like earlier robbers, they had little respect and often unwrapped mummies in search of souvenirs. They definitely deserved to have been cursed!

WAS THIS MUMMY (below) shrieking a curse when he died? If he was, he was cursing those who were killing him, for his expression suggests he was buried alive. Was he executed? Criminals' bodies were wrapped in sheepskin—so was his.

The "Screaming Mummy"

Fact or fiction?

STORIES ABOUT Egyptian mummies returning to life existed well before Carter found Tutankhamun's tomb. Edgar Allan Poe and Sir Arthur Conan Doyle, the creator of Sherlock Holmes, were among the authors who wrote spooky tales involving mummies. In the 1930s, audiences flocked to see films like *The Mummy*, in which Boris Karloff, who starred as the mummy, comes back to life after being entombed like the "screaming mummy" (right).

IN *THE MUMMY* Boris Karloff's appearance was based on Ramses III's mummy. The star lived to be 82, suffering no mummy's curse!

Ramses III

Boris Karloff in The Mummy

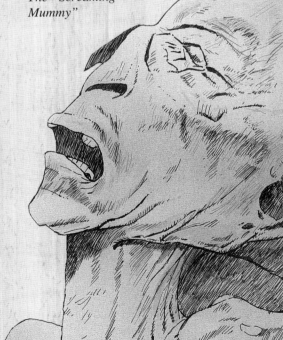

45

GREENLAND'S MUMMIES

EGYPT IS NOT the only country where mummified bodies have been found. In 1972 two men out hunting near Qilakitsoq on Greenland's west coast discovered two graves. One contained the bodies of three women, the other three women and two children. All the bodies were perfectly mummified and their clothing showed that they belonged to the Inuit people who settled in Greenland around AD 1000. Unlike ancient Egyptian mummies, these bodies had mummified naturally in Greenland's harsh climate.

Qilakitsoq, burial site of the Greenland mummies

Mini mummies!

SCIENTIFIC examination dated the bodies to about AD 1475. The examination also found another mummy: a perfectly preserved head louse! It's not surprising the Inuit had these parasites. In Greenland's climate they needed many layers of clothes for warmth—ideal breeding places for lice!

A mummified child

A Frozen Family?

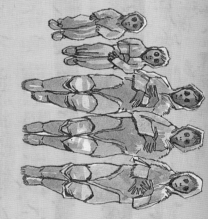

WHEN THE BODIES were put in the graves, they were laid on top of each other. Maybe this was because digging large graves was difficult in ground that was frozen for much of the year.

BOTH CHILDREN were boys: one was about 4, the other a six-month-old baby. The baby is the best preserved, perhaps because the wind and cold dried his small body more quickly than the larger ones.

FOUR OF THE women had patterns tattooed on their faces which only showed up in infrared photographs. The tattooing was possibly a sign of their status in Inuit society. All six had worn and damaged teeth, perhaps the result of years of chewing tough sealskin to soften it and make it usable for clothing.

Chewing sealskin

Tattoos

Reconstructed face of a Greenland mummy

Sealskin underclothing

Hood of parka

The mummies' boots

Fur-lined parka

Parka's long "tail"

Withstanding all conditions

THE BODIES WERE dressed as they would have been in life. In addition, the graves held a total of 78 more pieces of clothing, including 24 sealskin parkas. Because the mummies were well preserved, reconstructing the clothes was not difficult. Inuit parkas have changed little in several hundred years, showing just how well designed they are. The boots have soles sewn onto skin legs. All the skins, and the thread for sewing them, had to be chewed to make them flexible before they could be used—perhaps by these women themselves.

FROZEN IN TIME

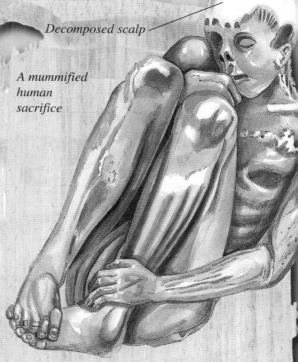

Decomposed scalp

A mummified human sacrifice

Silver llama found with a mummy in the Andes

THE BODIES OF the Inuit women were natural mummies, preserved by Greenland's climate. But they had been given a proper burial—the extra clothes show that. Some other naturally mummified bodies seem to suggest an unnatural death. Many such mummies come from the Andes mountains of South America. Archeologists believe the bodies belonged to people who were sacrificed to the gods and left on the mountains, where the wind and cold mummified them.

A peaceful death?

THIS BOY (above) looks peaceful. Was he drugged before being sacrificed and left in the Andes? A **cairn** of stones had been built around him to protect his body—the ground was too rocky for digging a grave. Only the top of his skull was exposed, and there his flesh has decayed.

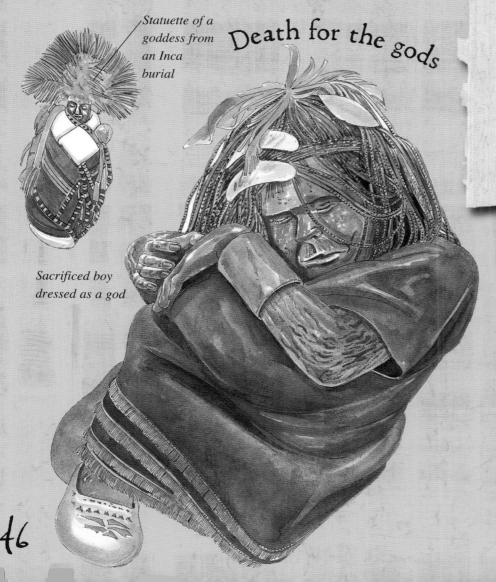

Statuette of a goddess from an Inca burial

Death for the gods

Sacrificed boy dressed as a god

Human sacrifice

THE **INCAS'** WEALTH came from the gold and silver mines around their capital, near Cuzco in modern Peru. The jewelry and gold-fringed clothes on this boy's mummified body (left) suggest he was sacrificed to an important god. Did he know his fate? We don't know. The **Aztecs** and **Maya** also practiced human sacrifice, and we know that the victims enjoyed a very good time for their last few weeks of life.

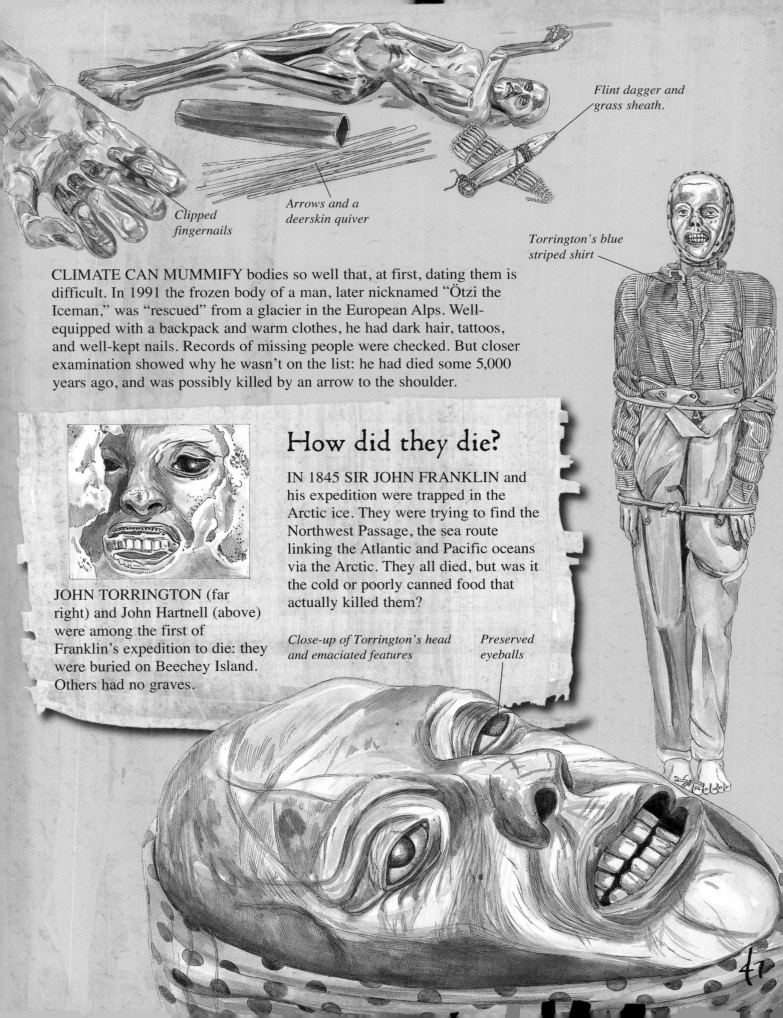

Flint dagger and grass sheath.

Clipped fingernails

Arrows and a deerskin quiver

Torrington's blue striped shirt

CLIMATE CAN MUMMIFY bodies so well that, at first, dating them is difficult. In 1991 the frozen body of a man, later nicknamed "Ötzi the Iceman," was "rescued" from a glacier in the European Alps. Well-equipped with a backpack and warm clothes, he had dark hair, tattoos, and well-kept nails. Records of missing people were checked. But closer examination showed why he wasn't on the list: he had died some 5,000 years ago, and was possibly killed by an arrow to the shoulder.

How did they die?

IN 1845 SIR JOHN FRANKLIN and his expedition were trapped in the Arctic ice. They were trying to find the Northwest Passage, the sea route linking the Atlantic and Pacific oceans via the Arctic. They all died, but was it the cold or poorly canned food that actually killed them?

JOHN TORRINGTON (far right) and John Hartnell (above) were among the first of Franklin's expedition to die: they were buried on Beechey Island. Others had no graves.

Close-up of Torrington's head and emaciated features

Preserved eyeballs

41

THE BOG PEOPLE

Victim's leather cap preserved by the bog

NORTHWESTERN EUROPE is not hot and has few high mountains, but it has mummies. Why? Because it has peat bogs. Oxygen, like heat, rots the soft parts of a body. By keeping out oxygen you can preserve a body—and a peat bog's spongy layers prevent oxygen reaching anything buried in it. Peat was used as a fuel in northwest Europe and many bodies were discovered in the bogs by peat diggers. Not all the deaths had been accidental!

Preserved by peat

TOLLUND MAN was found in a Danish bog. He had been hanged before being thrown into the bog and was naked except for the cap on his head and the hangman's noose still around his neck. Was he a criminal or a sacrifice?

Grauballe Man's foot

GRAUBALLE MAN'S face (above) looks flat because peat bogs are acidic and eat away the bones. He lived in Iron Age Denmark and had died of a savagely cut throat. What the bogs didn't destroy were details on the skin. Like many bog people, Grauballe Man's fingerprints are as clear as when he was alive.

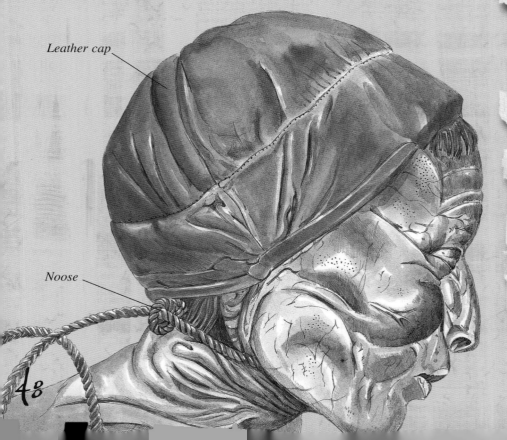

Leather cap

Noose

Grauballe Man's hand

A terrible death

ABOUT 2,000 YEARS ago a 14-year-old girl from Windeby, northern Germany, had a very unpleasant death. Archeologists think she must have been a criminal, because her head was half shaved and she was blindfolded before being thrown into a bog. But what makes her death really gruesome is that stones and tree branches had been tied to her body, weighing her down and giving her no chance of getting out. The Windeby Girl's skin looks very brown and leathery. This is due to the bog in which she died. The acidity of peat tans the skin, besides eating away bones.

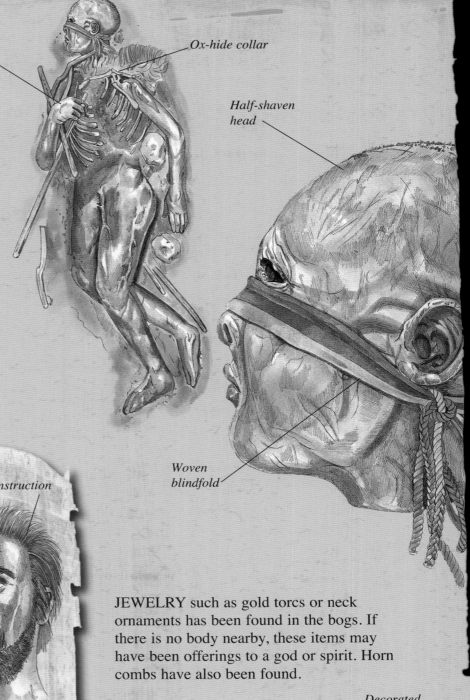

The Windeby Girl

Ox-hide collar

Half-shaven head

Woven blindfold

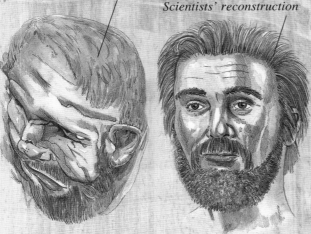

Lindow Man's distorted face

Scientists' reconstruction

Lindow Man

LINDOW MAN, nicknamed "Pete Marsh," was discovered in Cheshire, northwest England, in 1984. His death around 100 BC had been violent. He had been struck on the head three times, his jugular vein was severed, and then he was strangled. Finally he was thrown into the bog. After the bones had gone, the pressure of the peat distorted his face (above left). But forensic evidence suggests how he looked when alive (above right).

JEWELRY such as gold torcs or neck ornaments has been found in the bogs. If there is no body nearby, these items may have been offerings to a god or spirit. Horn combs have also been found.

Decorated horn comb

Gold torcs

PRESERVED ANIMALS

Fly preserved naturally in amber

THE ANCIENT Egyptians weren't the only people to preserve animals. Hunters have preserved them as trophies. Zoos preserve rare ones to study. Other animals have been mummified naturally: Cold climates work just as effectively on an animal's body as a human's. The coldest part of the Earth (apart from Antarctica) is Siberia. This huge region, about one twelfth of the Earth's surface, runs across the far north of Europe and Asia. There is little food there now for large land animals, but there must have been plenty once. How do we know? From the mummified remains of woolly mammoths.

ALTHOUGH THIS BABY mammoth died about 44,000 years ago, it was preserved, deep frozen, by the Siberian cold. It is not the only mammoth found there. Adults, complete with their skin and hair, have survived. Such remains are fragile and sudden exposure can destroy them.

Frozen for 40,000 years!

40,000 years old and he's still hairy!

He looks good for his age!

Chi-Chi the panda

FOR MANY YEARS Chi-Chi the giant panda was a favorite with visitors to London Zoo. These animals are in danger of extinction, so when she died in 1972 her body was thoroughly studied. Then it was preserved and is now in the Natural History Museum, London.

Bamboo shoots

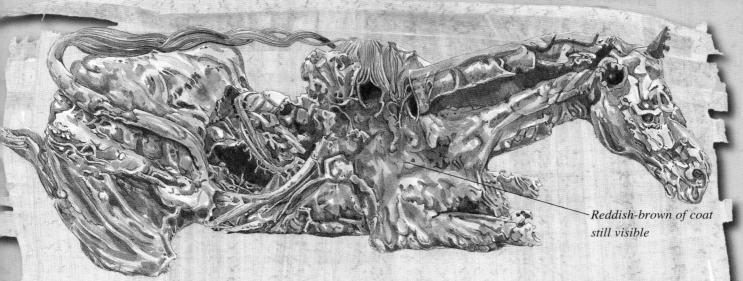

Reddish-brown of coat
still visible

THIS HORSE WAS KILLED by a blow to its head and preserved in the cold of Siberia. It was found in a tomb in the Altai Mountains on the borders of Russia and Kazakhstan. It belonged to a **Scythian** chief who lived there about 2,500 years ago.

The Scythians were great horsemen and warriors. When a chief died, his body was embalmed and then buried with goods for the next life. At least one of his horses was put in the tomb to help him on his journey.

Mummification or taxidermy?

TAXIDERMY IS the cleaning, stuffing, and mounting of birds and animals. It was popular in Victorian times, when many homes had stuffed animals and birds as ornaments. The real skill of a taxidermist lies in making the dead creature look as natural and lifelike as possible. Hunters also use taxidermists to turn the animals they've killed into trophies. Animals that have been preserved like this are not really mummies. All that is preserved is their skin, which is usually hung over an artificial body, although the skull and leg bones are sometimes kept to support the skin. Freeze-drying bodies in a vacuum chamber is a new method of preservation—but natural Siberian cold was just as effective.

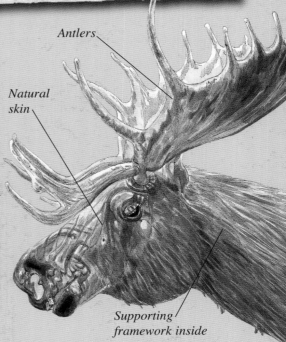

Antlers

Natural
skin

Supporting
framework inside

A Victorian tableau called "Schoolmaster's Severity"

Stuffed for show

A THOROUGHLY unnatural example of the taxidermist's work, the animals' "school room" (left) was shown at the Great Exhibition in London in 1851.

NEW "LIVES" FOR OLD

The brandy used to preserve Nelson worked so well that a cast could be made of his face

AS WE KNOW, when a person dies the body starts rotting. If bodies are left lying around they quickly become health hazards. So the dead are usually disposed of quickly. They may be buried, cremated, or put in special places for animals or birds to pick their bones clean. But, just occasionally, dead people have new "lives." Bodies can be preserved by traditional methods, such as embalming. Could anyone really be brought back to life? It doesn't seem likely—but once it seemed a fantasy that humans would walk on the moon!

Plastination

IN 1978, controversial german scientist Gunther von Hagens unveiled a new method of preserving a body—plastination. The method involves replacing the fat and water naturally found in a body with a special form of plastic. These hard, odorless "mummies" have not only been used for scientific study—some have also been displayed as works of art.

I think it's horrible!

I think it's a masterpiece!

Nelson's barrel

When British admiral Lord Nelson died in 1805 at the Battle of Trafalgar, his body was brought back to England.

Nelson's body was preserved for the long trip—in a barrel of brandy!

After his journey, Nelson's body was transferred to a lead coffin and he was given a proper funeral. The brandy was drunk by his crew!

IT'S OFTEN the rich and eccentric who want new "lives." Gala Dalí, wife of the artist Salvador Dalí, wanted to die at home. She didn't, so her body was dressed and driven back to their house to fulfill her wish.

Gala Dalí

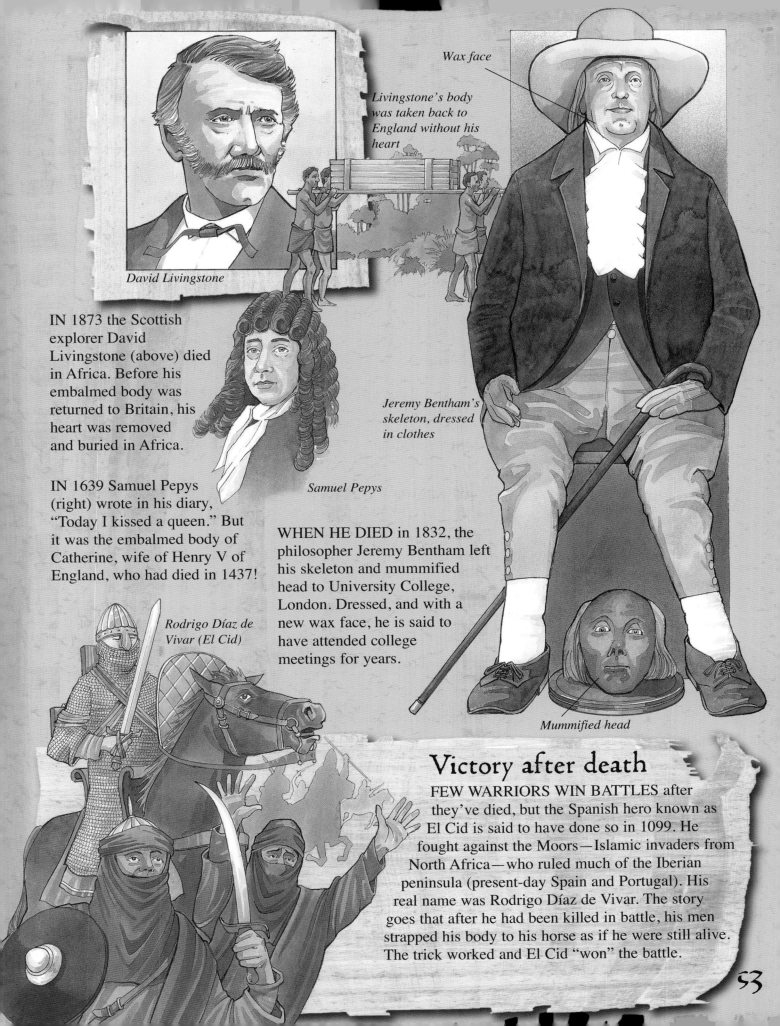

David Livingstone

Wax face

Livingstone's body was taken back to England without his heart

IN 1873 the Scottish explorer David Livingstone (above) died in Africa. Before his embalmed body was returned to Britain, his heart was removed and buried in Africa.

Jeremy Bentham's skeleton, dressed in clothes

Samuel Pepys

IN 1639 Samuel Pepys (right) wrote in his diary, "Today I kissed a queen." But it was the embalmed body of Catherine, wife of Henry V of England, who had died in 1437!

WHEN HE DIED in 1832, the philosopher Jeremy Bentham left his skeleton and mummified head to University College, London. Dressed, and with a new wax face, he is said to have attended college meetings for years.

Rodrigo Díaz de Vivar (El Cid)

Mummified head

Victory after death

FEW WARRIORS WIN BATTLES after they've died, but the Spanish hero known as El Cid is said to have done so in 1099. He fought against the Moors—Islamic invaders from North Africa—who ruled much of the Iberian peninsula (present-day Spain and Portugal). His real name was Rodrigo Díaz de Vivar. The story goes that after he had been killed in battle, his men strapped his body to his horse as if he were still alive. The trick worked and El Cid "won" the battle.

IS THAT A BODY?

The Turin Shroud (above) was believed to show Jesus Christ's face. In 1988 carbon dating showed that the cloth was likely to be medieval.

S OME BODIES are not what they seem. Even ancient Egyptian embalmers sometimes cheated. If a body, or even part of a body, had been lost or damaged, they'd use something else—after all, the bandages hid everything. But modern technology makes faking difficult. "Piltdown Man" (below, right) was trumpeted as the "missing link" between modern humans and their earlier ancestors when it was first discovered in 1912. If it had been discovered today, it would quickly have been seen as a fraud.

A hoax 'mermaid'

WHEN THE VOLCANO Vesuvius erupted in AD 79, volcanic ash buried the city of Pompeii, killing every living thing. Although the bodies rotted, they left spaces in the hardened ash which had surrounded them. This plaster cast was made from the space left by a dead dog.

Plaster cast of a dog

Fantastical fakes

STORIES of mermaids and mermen are common, but their bodies are rare. Is this body proof that they exist? No! A hoaxer joined a monkey's body to a fish's tail.

The living dead!

STORIES of vampires and other "undead" creatures have been told for centuries. At one time, people really believed in them.

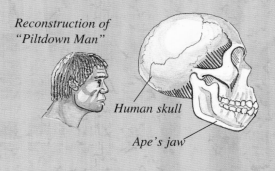

Reconstruction of "Piltdown Man"

Human skull

Ape's jaw

"PILTDOWN MAN," found in 1912, consisted of a human skull and an ape's jaw (above). The fraud was not exposed until 1953.

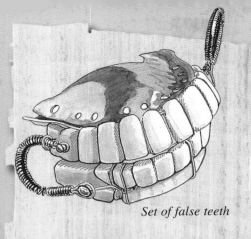

Set of false teeth

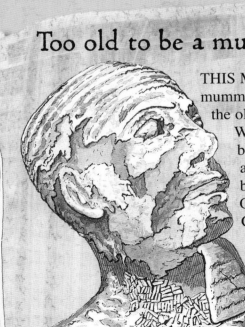

Jade body suit

IN THE 2ND CENTURY BC a Chinese noble and his wife were buried in magnificent suits of jade and gold (right). But, in spite of their wealth, their bodies rotted like the poorest peasant's.

UNTIL PHOTOGRAPHY was invented in the 19th century, a **death mask** (a plaster cast) was the most accurate way to record a person's likeness. Below is the death mask of the poet John Keats (1795–1821).

A secondhand set

LEGEND HAS IT that President George Washington (1732–1799), wore false teeth made of wood. Actually, they were made from human and animal teeth. Human teeth were often obtained from corpses, or from the mouths of the very poor, who sold them.

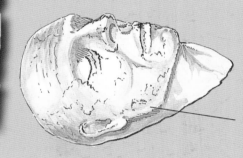

Death mask of John Keats

King Charles II

Mummy or dummy?

CHARLES II was king of England from 1660 to 1685. When he died, a wax effigy of him (left) stood on his coffin as his body lay in state in Whitehall, London. Then it was laid on the coffin as his funeral procession traveled through the streets of London.

Too old to be a mummy!

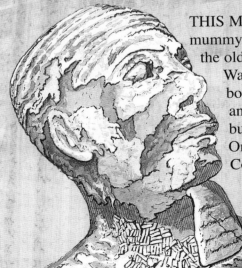

THIS MAY BE the oldest Egyptian mummy, but it no longer contains the oldest Egyptian body. Poor Waty—he paid to have his body embalmed, mummified, and buried around 2400 BC, but it decomposed long ago. Only the wrappings remain. Coated in plaster and resin, they have set into a cast—but they do show what he looked like.

LASTING MEMORIALS

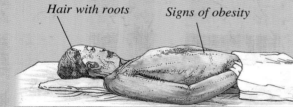

Tattoo on the arm of a Scythian chief

BECAUSE THE ANCIENT Egyptians were powerful for so long and left so many mummies, we often forget that other peoples, in other times and places, also mummified their dead. Why? For many reasons: respect for the dead, to help them in a new life, to ensure something of a much-loved person remained. Headhunters in South America and New Guinea mummified the heads of their victims as trophies.

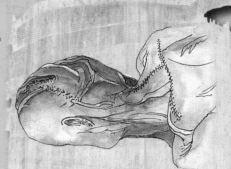

Still stitched

WHEN THIS SIBERIAN woman (above) was embalmed more than a thousand years ago, her skull was opened to remove her brain. The embalmer's neat stitches where the skin was sewn back are still visible.

Hair with roots *Signs of obesity* *Supple joints* *Good skin*

Lady Dai

Bodyguards ?

Preserved bodies guarding a village in Papua New Guinea

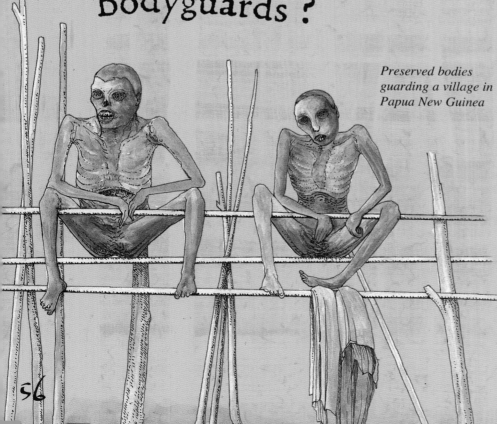

Salt and charcoal?

TWO THOUSAND years ago the Chinese noblewoman Lady Dai (above, left) died. Her body was preserved with salt and buried in a nest of coffins packed with charcoal. She is so well preserved that her joints are still supple.

LOOK AFTER YOUR ancestors and they'll look after you. These preserved bodies (left), perched on a frame guarding a village in Papua New Guinea, were smoked and then covered in clay.

Shrunken head

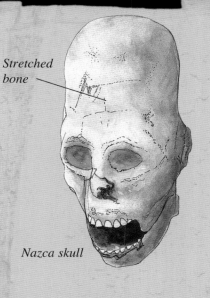

Stretched bone

Nazca skull

Peru's mummies

THESE STONE TOMBS were discovered on a mountainside in Peru. The bodies inside had been mummified and supplied with plenty of food—just as in ancient Egypt.

THIS TROPHY was once the head of an enemy of the Jivaro Indians of Ecuador, South America. After the head had been cut off, the skull was removed, which is why the head is so small. Finally the remains were dried and decorated.

THE NAZCA PEOPLE, who lived in southern Peru from about 200 BC to AD 500, carefully embalmed their dead. This skull's odd shape was not caused by the embalmers, but by the Nazca custom of binding babies' heads soon after birth.

Mummified body held at the Convent of the Capuchins

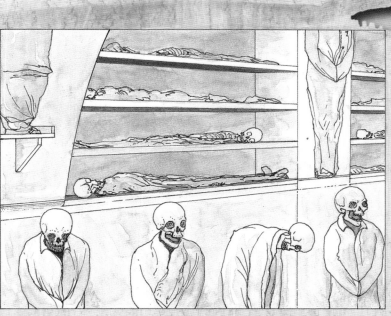

IN PALERMO, SICILY, mummifying bodies went on until 1881. The catacombs (underground cemetery) of the city's Convent of the Capuchins held hundreds of bodies. The embalming, which was done by the monks, began in the 16th century. Wealthy people reserved places in the catacombs long before they died. There they stood or lay, awaiting the Last Judgment.

SEPARATE LIVES

JT IS NOT JUST BODIES that have enjoyed lives after death. Even parts of some corpses have had lives of their own, sometimes because it was too difficult to preserve the whole body. Portions of the bodies of saints were especially popular with Christian churches and monasteries. If a church had even a small part of a saint, they would be sure of attracting hundreds of pilgrims—and their money, too. Sometimes heads were preserved separately—to prove that the owners were dead!

Skull of 6000 BC from Jericho, covered in plaster modeled like a face with shell "eyes"

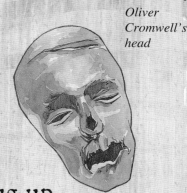

Oliver Cromwell's head

Dug up

WHEN BRITISH revolutionary leader Oliver Cromwell died in 1658, his body was buried. But after Charles II came to the throne in 1660, Cromwell's enemies dug up his body to display his head in public.

Reliquary said to hold the finger of "Doubting" Thomas

Reliquary containing St. Andrew's foot, now known to be a fake

Religious relics

THE BIGGER THE BETTER, or so the Christian church believed in the Middle Ages. The foot made of gold on top of the richly jeweled **reliquary** (above) shows the body part inside: the foot of St. Andrew. Sadly, modern science shows that many such **relics** are neither ancient nor human.

THOMAS, ONE OF JESUS' DISCIPLES, is nicknamed "Doubting" because he did not believe Jesus had died and then risen from the dead. After thrusting a finger into one of Jesus' wounds, his doubt turned to belief. The reliquary (left) is said to hold that finger.

THE HEART of Robert Bruce, Scotland's most famous king, had an adventurous life. The king wanted it taken to the **Holy Land** after his death. When he died in 1329, Sir James Douglas set off with it. Sadly, Douglas started fighting in Spain, and is said to have thrown away the casket and the heart in battle.

Sir James Douglas

Book bound in human skin

"Waterloo teeth"

"Waterloo teeth"

TEETH, AS WE'VE SEEN, often led new lives as sets of false teeth. Many such teeth came from the bodies of dead soldiers and were nicknamed "Waterloo" teeth, after the famous battle of Waterloo.

Bound in skin!

FEW BOOKS are bound in human skin like the one above. It's macabre but appropriate, because the book is about the dissection of the body of John Horwood, a 19th-century murderer. The gibbet on the cover shows how he died.

VICTOR FRANKENSTEIN'S monster (above), made of body parts, is the subject of Mary Shelley's 1818 novel and the inspiration for many films.

MODERN MUMMIES

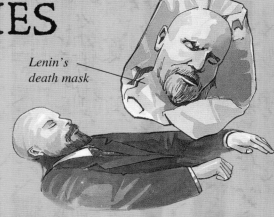

Lenin's death mask

Eva Perón (above and opposite page) was embalmed in 1952

MOST OF THE mummies in this book are ancient, but that definitely doesn't mean that embalming and mummification belong to the past. It's just that these processes are not as common as they once were. But the reasons for embalming are much the same as they were for the ancient Egyptians and other cultures: political or cultural reasons, and (most importantly) the quest for the afterlife. But what is different is that some people now want their new life to be here on earth.

Lenin

Back in fashion?

AFTER HIS ASSASSINATION in 1865, the body of President Abraham Lincoln (below) was embalmed, making this ancient practice fashionable again.

PERHAPS THE MOST famous modern mummy is Vladimir Lenin's. A leader of the Russian Revolution that overthrew the Czar in 1918, Lenin became the first premier of the Soviet Union. When he died in 1924 his body was embalmed for display in a special mausoleum in Red Square, Moscow. It is maintained by skilled embalmers so it stays looking good.

Even presidents can be mummies!

President Abraham Lincoln

Preserved for a long trip

DURING THE CIVIL WAR (1861–1865) soldiers' bodies were embalmed (below) so they could be sent home for burial—it was the only practical thing to do before refrigeration was invented.

Draining off body fluids

Lost and found

THANKS TO her social reforms, Eva Perón, second wife of Juan Perón the president of Argentina, was very popular with the country's poor. After she died of cancer in 1952 her body was embalmed. But she remained so popular that when her husband was overthrown in 1955, her body in its silver coffin was conveniently "lost" by the new government. Juan Perón became president again in 1973, but died in exile in 1974. By then Eva's coffin had been "found" again, and husband and wife were reunited.

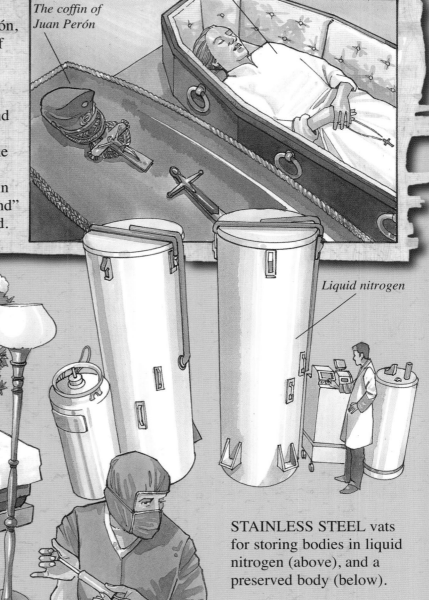

Eva Perón

The coffin of Juan Perón

Liquid nitrogen

STAINLESS STEEL vats for storing bodies in liquid nitrogen (above), and a preserved body (below).

Flowers and soft lighting add to the dignified, restful atmosphere.

MANY PEOPLE'S BODIES (above) are embalmed and put on display before their funeral.

LIQUID NITROGEN, used to preserve today's rich, is a long way from the natron, scented herbs, and resin used to embalm the rich in ancient Egypt. Will the nitrogen be more, or less, effective? What will remain in 3,000 years' time? We don't know. All we can be sure of is that none of us will be around to find out!

61

GLOSSARY

amulet a small charm believed to give protection from evil.

Anubis the ancient Egyptian jackal-headed god of the underworld.

Aztecs a people of what is now Mexico, conquered by the Spanish in the 16th century.

ba a person's character.

Book of the Dead a collection of prayers and spells to help the dead in the afterlife.

cairn a mound of stones built as a memorial.

Canopic jars jars to hold a mummy's internal organs.

death mask a plaster cast of a dead person's face.

dirge a mournful song in memory of the dead.

faience a glasslike material made of powdered quartz.

forensic using science or technology to establish a fact.

hieroglyphs symbols used in the sacred writings of ancient Egypt.

Holy Land the area of the Middle East where Christians believe Jesus Christ lived.

Horus the god of the sun in his morning aspect.

Inca a people of the central and southern Andes, conquered by Spaniards in the 16th century.

Inuit a people of Greenland, northern Canada, and Alaska.

Isis the Ancient Egyptian goddess of fertility and wife of Osiris.

ka a person's life force or spirit.

Lower Egypt the Nile valley from the Mediterranean Sea to Cairo.

Maya a people who lived in Central America from about 1000 BC to AD 1000.

Middle Kingdom the period in ancient Egyptian history from *c*.2040 to 1640 BC.

natron a natural form of salt often used to preserve bodies.

New Kingdom the period in ancient Egyptian history from *c*.1550 to 1070 BC.

Old Kingdom the period in ancient Egyptian history from *c*.2575 to 2134 BC.

Osiris the ancient Egyptian god of the dead.

papyrus a reed growing beside the Nile, used by the ancient Egyptians to make paper.

professional mourners women paid to join funeral processions to wail and lament the dead.

quartzite a hard rock mostly made of quartz.

relic an article or remains that once belonged to a holy person.

reliquary a container for relics.

resin sap that oozes from the trunks of some pine and fir trees.

sarcophagus a stone coffin.

scarab a dung beetle; an ancient Egyptian symbol of the sun.

scribe a professional writer—an important person in societies where few could read or write.

Scythians a nomadic people who lived north of the Black Sea from the 8th to 3rd centuries BC.

shroud the cloth in which a body is wrapped and buried.

silt very fine soil deposited on land when a river floods.

Sobek the ancient Egyptian god of water.

taxidermy the cleaning, stuffing, and mounting of a dead animal.

Thoth the ancient Egyptian god of wisdom and writing.

Upper Egypt the Nile valley roughly from Cairo in the north to Aswan in the south.

INDEX

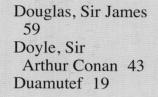

MUMMY FACTS

Why "mummy"? The word "mummy" comes from the Persian word *mummiya*, meaning bitumen or pitch. Badly made Egyptian mummies were embalmed in resin, which blackened over time, leading to the incorrect belief that bitumen was the embalming agent.

Sweet king Not all early mummies were embalmed with salts and bandages. The body of Alexander the Great is said to have been on show for years in a glass coffin filled with honey. We can't be sure that this was true, but we do know that honey acts as a preservative.

Relative values Visiting the family was certainly an interesting trip for the people of old Palermo in Sicily. Residents would regularly go and picnic with their mummified relations at the Capuchin convent, changing their clothes and discussing family matters with them—just as if they were still alive.

Cat-astrophe An ancient cemetery filled with embalmed cats was discovered at Beni Hasan in Egypt during the 19th century. They were not considered important or valuable at the time, so they were shipped to England and processed to make fertilizers.

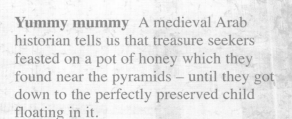

Yummy mummy A medieval Arab historian tells us that treasure seekers feasted on a pot of honey which they found near the pyramids – until they got down to the perfectly preserved child floating in it.

Culture clash In 1978, sand-mummified bodies were discovered on the edge of the Gobi Desert in China. The mummies suggest that the Chinese were in contact with Bronze Age Europeans, despite the Chinese tradition that their civilization was free from all outside influences.